trish's french kitcnen

trish's french kitchen

TRISH DESEINE

photography by Deirdre Rooney

KYLE BOOKS

This edition published in 2011 by
Kyle Books
23 Howland Street
London W1T 4AY
general.enquiries@kylebooks.com
www.kylebooks.com

First published in Great Britain in 2008 by
Kyle Cathie Limited

ISBN 978 0 85783 020 3

Text © 2008 Trish Deseine
Design © 2008 Kyle Books
Photographs © 2008 Deirdre Rooney

Project editor Suzanna de Jong
Photographer Deirdre Rooney
Designer Nicky Collings
Stylists Alisa Morov and Agnes Bouchier-Hayes
Copy editor Lesley Levene
Proofreader Caroline Ball
Indexer Anna Norman
Production Sha Huxtable and Linda Sima

Trish Deseine is hereby identified as the author of this
work in accordance with Section 77 of the Copyright,
Designs and Patents Act 1988.

A Cataloguing in Publication record for this title is
available from the British Library.

Colour reproduction by Sang Choy
Printed and bound in Singapore by Tien Wah Press

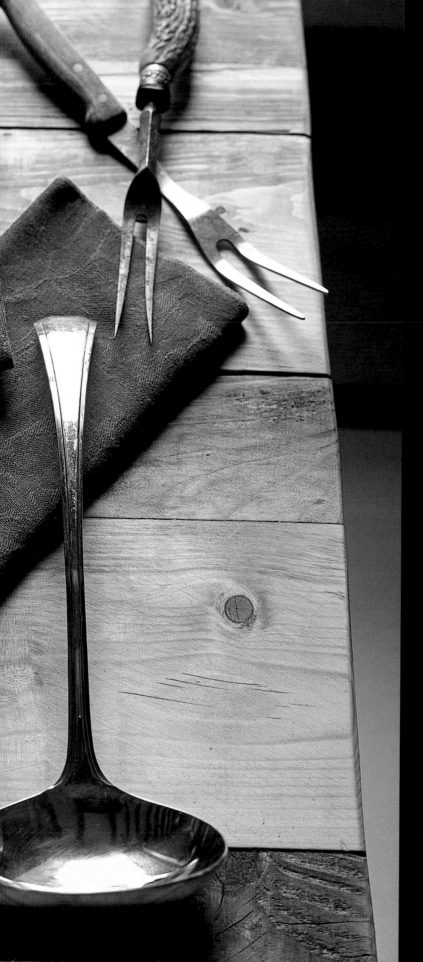

contents

INTRODUCTION

In the twenty years I have lived in France, I've had the luxury and good fortune to develop my French cooking skills in the wonderful kitchens of my three French homes. My Paris kitchen is six floors up without a lift, so certainly dictates careful menu planning and shopping – I find myself making lists. Set in the middle of a typically busy part of Paris, I have everything I need at the foot of my building, but those stairs... This kitchen is right in the heart of the innovative French food culture, where shops and new restaurants are opening all the time. My cooking is experimental – here I am looking for taste experiences, I bring ideas home, try out new techniques and different combinations. A new restaurant craze is to make creams and foams, so recently I got out my syphon and experimented on some willing friends. I keep my *verrines* here, the little glasses I use for serving individual portions, which you see in restaurants and at cocktail parties all over the city. A current favourite is the recipe for *verrines* filled with sweet potato and crab. My friends gather in my Paris kitchen for long drawn-out evenings with food and conversation. I make an effort with presentation and decor, put flowers on the table, always a tablecloth, and some pretty candles. In my Paris kitchen, I entertain the French way, and you'll find examples of these kinds of dishes in the POSH chapter of this book.

In St Germain-en-Laye, a leafy suburb just west of Paris, you'll find me in my family kitchen, where quick, nutritious weekday suppers and cosy Sunday lunches happen. My kids have their own social lives now, so I gain a few of their friends on most occasions. Here I keep things dissociated, serving everything separately to allow for all the different likes and dislikes. The family kitchen is about feeding people, not about impressing them, and the recipes in my FAST chapter are perfect for it. Every piece of equipment has its place there. I don't have the cooker of my dreams yet, and make do with a camping stove, believe it or not, but I have a great oven, and it is compact. There's no question of a second set of anything here – there is one of everything, and it is all in constant use. The kitchen is the heart of the house, the way cooking is the heart of life. Everything seems to revolve around it.

In Bonnevilliers, halfway between Paris and Rouen, my country kitchen was a proper room, looking out over the courtyard and the herb garden outside. Although I no longer spend time there, it has left its traces in this book, especially in the SLOW and LARDER chapters. This is where I learned to cook quintessential French stews and roasts, make compotes, big salads and a lot of fruit tarts. The beautiful big oven was great for cakes, and would also house a couple of shoulders of lamb or a large turkey. It was a light place, with a pale yellow floor and the most beautiful built-in cabinets and cupboards with mirrors and glass. We left everything as we found it when we bought the house, all we added was the cooker and a butcher's block. The kitchen became a family room, the hub of the house, where everyone gathered. In this kitchen, time slowed down. Its sheer size allowed for a typical French feast; there was enough room to store the shopping for a whole week, including provisions for a dinner party on the Saturday night. There was real feeling of abundance and plenty when I spent time there. The Normandy fish casserole and *la potée Lorraine* recipes are favourites from that time in my life.

No matter what kitchen I'm in, it's about sitting down and spending time with friends and family – this is a vital part of the French food culture. Even though French cuisine is changing and evolving, their love of food and the quality of what they eat haven't. The French are conscious of all the elements that go into making our food: the air, sun and soil, the altitude and orientation of the land from which it comes. The combination of these elements is what the French call *terroir*, a word that, tellingly, has no English translation. *Terroir* is about the knowledge of the producers, the tradition of the product's name, and the geographical region it comes from. If a particular region is associated with a certain food, that has to be protected. For example, Camembert cheese can only be made in Camembert. To protect the foods that are France's monuments, there is the *appellation d'origine controlée* (AOC), a label controlled by a national institute, protecting the quality, authenticity and regionality of a product. Chickens from Bresse, mussels from Mont St Michel, chestnuts from the Ardèche, walnuts from Grenoble, green lentils from Puy, *piment d'Espelette*, the list of certified foods is endless.

Nowadays, mastering French cooking at home is a state of mind to aspire to, not a list of instructions to follow. It wasn't always like this, but the rules aren't quite so strict any more. In fact, when you really look at the principles of what makes French cooking French, it has little to do with its image of elegant, fine dining with extremely sophisticated food. French cooking is much more about the quality and the origin and the goodness of what you're eating. There is much more variety to be found in what my generation cooks at home. My peers are more adventurous, willing to try out new things, taking inspiration not only from their ancestors but also from foreign cuisines and applying what they've learned to their own creations.

The dishes in this book follow mood and desire, not geography and history. Chapters such as FAST and SLOW reflect the pace of life at different moments in time, while sometimes it's occasions that dictate what's on the menu, like in POSH. In the RAW chapter, there's the opportunity to celebrate France's incredible produce in a minimal way, allowing natural flavours to shine through. The recipes in SWEET will soothe when only something sugary will do, and in LARDER you will find reasons why it's ok to leave that big shop for another day. I have found this a much more natural way of organising the recipes, one that reflects the open approach the French have to cooking and food.

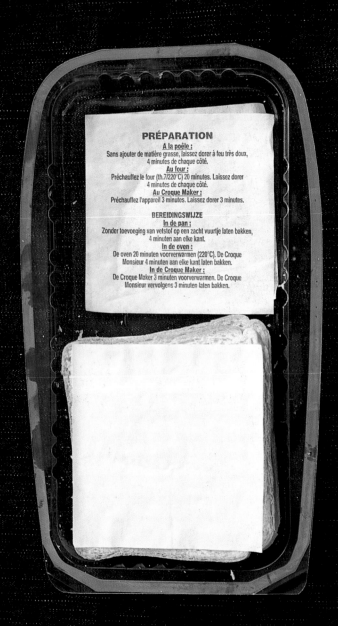

PRÉPARATION

À la poêle :
Sans ajouter de matière grasse, laissez dorer à feu très doux,
4 minutes de chaque côté.
Au four :
Préchauffez le four (th.7/220°C) 20 minutes. Laissez dorer
4 minutes de chaque côté.
Au Croque Maker :
Préchauffez l'appareil 3 minutes. Laissez dorer 3 minutes.

BEREIDINGSWIJZE

In de pan :
Zonder toevoeging van vetstof op een zacht vuurtje laten bakken,
4 minuten aan elke kant.
In de oven :
De oven 20 minuten voorverwarmen (220°C). De Croque
Monsieur 4 minuten aan elke kant laten bakken.
In de Croque Maker :
De Croque Maker 3 minuten voorverwarmen. De Croque
Monsieur vervolgens 3 minuten laten bakken.

Many of the recipes in this chapter involve vegetables, fruit and fish, and are the types of dishes I would rustle up quickly for lunch after coming home a little late from the market, or in the evenings when my children's homework has dragged on. These are a mixture of open-a-tin, quick assembly and cooked-from-scratch recipes, where the speed of the cooking methods is certainly convenient on a busy day.

Equipment-wise, your greatest allies for fast, healthy cooking are a saucepan with a steamer, a heavy cast-iron pan and a good oven. The recipes in this chapter keep the number of saucepans and hob rings needed to a minimum. They are dishes that cook in the time it takes to prepare them or that can be left alone after the preparation for the oven or hob to do the work for you. I hope they will help you consider 'fast' food not just as opening a pre-cooked pack from your freezer. In French kitchens, you won't find much in the way of convenience food. There is always a better way! It comes down to shopping sensibly, introducing one or two basic items to your weekly shopping list, like beautiful cherry tomatoes, crunchy apples or a good French cheese – fresh things that will stay in your fridge for a while and can be considered a snack as well as an addition to an unavoidably starch-inclusive main meal.

These can still be very sociable recipes, as they are easy to cook with your friends around you in the kitchen, but they're certainly not just to be relegated to weekday refuelling – they are certainly elegant enough to feed dinner guests. The quick cooking time liberates the mind so you can focus on your guests and let the evening commence.

So, unlike the recipes in the next chapter, SLOW, where layers of taste get cooked on to each other, here cooking a few ingredients fast and fresh gives a pure and simple taste. When you haven't hours and hours to shop and cook, these recipes fit themselves into your life rather than the other way around, and are the best way I've found to grow young muscle and bone whilst not seeming to invade busy lives.

FAST

MUSHROOM & SPINACH SOUP WITH GARLIC BREAD

The first time I ate garlic bread (and indeed garlic) was in an Italian restaurant in Belfast. I was fourteen and thought it was fabulous – a fluffy warm baguette full of butter and nothing whatsoever to do with the original Italian peasant bruschetta, simple stale bread rubbed with garlic and soaked with olive oil. Like chicken tikka, another foreign creation of a non-indigenous dish, it became a popular and mistreated classic that is for some reason considered typically French.

Miraculously, my children love spinach. This hearty soup, fast to rustle up thanks to packet baby spinach, has also become the only way they will eat mushrooms. I try never to 'hide' ingredients in dishes, so everyone was warned from the outset that there were mushrooms in the soup, proving that it's the slippery texture of the mushrooms they don't like, not their taste. The garlic bread, on the other hand, is a completely selfish retro addition and was rejected out of hand by my three younger kids. They may be half French, but raw garlic remains too potent for their palates. I'll try again when they are fourteen.

For 4

25g butter
400g wild mushrooms, cleaned and chopped
225g baby spinach, washed
1 litre chicken stock
1 bouquet garni
salt and pepper

FOR THE GARLIC BREAD
150g butter, softened
4 garlic cloves, very finely chopped
a handful of parsley, roughly chopped
1 baguette

Melt the butter in a saucepan, add the mushrooms and cook gently for a minute or two until they brown.

Add the spinach and give it a stir or two. Cover the pan. Once the spinach has wilted, pour in the chicken stock, add the bouquet garni and bring to the boil.

Simmer for about 7–8 minutes until the mushrooms are softened, then remove the bouquet garni and blitz in a blender until smooth. Taste and adjust the seasoning.

To make the garlic bread, preheat the oven to 160°C/325°F/gas mark 3.

Mix the butter, garlic and parsley together. (You could also put the whole cloves in a mini blender with the butter and parsley and blitz until smooth.)

Halve the bread along the centre and spread both top and bottom with the garlic butter. Wrap in tin foil and put in the oven for 15 minutes.

Serve immediately with the hot soup.

CHICORY & BEER SOUP

This recipe is a nice example of the seepage between Belgian and French cooking. Brasseries first appeared in Belgium, and were traditionally places where you'd drink your beer, and some food was served alongside. Now they are first and foremost eateries and can be found all over Belgium and France.

Two of Belgium's most famous products come together in this unusual soup. Chicory is already a bit of an acquired taste and cooking heightens its bitterness, so the sugar in the recipe is very necessary. Another way of further balancing the flavours would be to serve the soup with the sweet, spicy Belgian biscuits known as speculoos.

For 2

25g butter

2 small shallots, finely chopped

4 heads fresh chicory, washed and roughly chopped

300ml chicken stock

150ml dark Belgian beer

1 tablespoon brown sugar

2–3 tablespoons single cream

2 rashers streaky bacon

salt and freshly ground black pepper

Melt the butter in a heavy-based saucepan, then sweat the shallots and the chicory until soft but not coloured.

Add the stock and the beer, bring to the boil and simmer for about 20 minutes.

Remove from the heat and blend until smooth. Add sugar to offset the bitterness and then the cream.

Fry the bacon until it is very crisp.

Season the soup with salt and pepper and serve immediately with the bacon rashers.

EASY (AND VERY LAZY) CASSOULET

Cassoulet is really an on-location-only dish, something to enjoy in Toulouse, Castelnaudry or Carcassonne, with your head bowed in respect for tradition and folklore. There are many versions of the dish, whose name comes from the *cassolo* or clay pot in which it was originally cooked, and all contain white beans or *lingots,* plus varying combinations of sausage, duck and goose confit, roast mutton, pork and sometimes even partridge.

However, much as I adore eating cassoulet at other people's tables, I am not one for making these two-day, labour-of-love, steeped-in-history dishes, especially when they involve the overnight soaking of pulses. What's more, I have never seen a recipe for real cassoulet that fills less than two pages. I prefer to speed things up a bit, which is perfectly possible as the French produce several of the necessary ingredients in tinned and bottled form – but do not be tempted to use anything that is not French.

For 4

150g bacon lardons
2 Toulouse sausages
1 onion, finely chopped
1 leek, finely chopped
olive oil (optional)
750g tin French *haricots blancs, haricots tarbais* or *lingots* in tomato sauce
3 legs of confit of duck

Heat a heavy-based frying pan. Add the bacon lardons and colour slightly, then add the sausages and fry gently until they are cooked through.

Sweat the onion and leek in the same pan, adding some oil if necessary.

Pour in the beans and bring to a slow simmer.

Heat the duck, in its fat, in a separate pan, drain and add to the sausages and beans.

Transfer to a clay dish and serve immediately. Or, as a nod to tradition, pop it into the oven at 180°C/350°F/gas mark 4 or under the grill and let the traditional golden crust form on top.

CORSICAN SAUSAGES

The Corsican *coppa*, *lonzu* and *figatellu* sausages are useful mainstays of my larder and my personal favourites when it comes to rustling up the fastest of meals. Thin slices of dark, moist *figatellu* are great with a glass of red wine to keep impromptu guests waiting while I cook something more filling, and an ingredient my kids love as sandwich fillers in last-minute packed lunches. Pale pink, paper-like slivers of *lonzu* are wonderful in summer, served with melons, apricots or peaches for a speedy starter, and also very good next to pineapple as a different take on the common or garden Hawaiian pizza. The deep-flavoured Corsican *coppa* has become extremely popular over the past five years or so. In my house, it now makes the cut in the tight choice of ham for a raclette, the ultimate fast feast. The little round slices seem to be just the right size to house the melted cheese and my kids love to build mini edible sculptures with a slice or two of potato before devouring them. I haven't the guts (or the space) to invest in a meat slicer, but it's very tempting when you taste the difference between pre-sliced and freshly sliced *charcuterie*.

Farming in Corsica is still a rustic, peasant tradition. Most of the sixty thousand 'domesticated' pigs on the island are in fact semi-wild, released to forage for food much of the year. Along with sheep and goats (and Corsicans) they are a huge road hazard, moving quickly between stretches of forest on this magnificently wild island. There, they feast on wild chestnuts, once the island's food staple, acorns and plants of the *maquis* – a dense bittersweet jungle of evergreen plants like myrtle, lavender, rosemary and thyme. This special diet gives the pork meat a unique flavour of nuts, sugar and herbs and a sharper taste than elsewhere in *saucisson*-mad France. Hence their great reputation for a wonderful taste and their prestigious status in the world of sausages. Luckily, lots of friends go to Corsica on holiday, and the *saucissons* are a favourite holiday souvenir, providing a steady supply to stock up my larder.

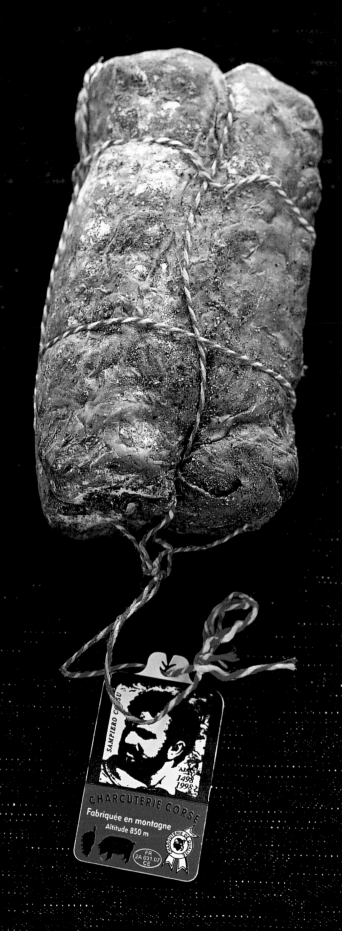

MACKEREL WITH PISTACHIO PESTO

Mackerel isn't much celebrated in France – it's considered a lesser fish and too smelly to cook at home. However, it's my children's favourite fish, and mackerel are abundant, cheap and full of goodness, so I cook them quite regularly. They are easy to tackle whole, juicy and flavoursome, and the brain food argument is an added bonus. Imagine getting better marks at school next day thanks to what you had for tea! I'm not great at barbecues, so my fish tends to get roasted in the oven or cooked in a griddle pan, but of course flames and smoke will enhance their taste even more. I always pay attention to what goes on the side: usually some warm potatoes, or a classic potato salad, and always a feisty salsa or pesto as a condiment to wake the dish up. Pistachios don't have a strong taste, so just a little garlic is called for in this recipe. I leave out the traditional basil and rely on lime zest and juice to give the pesto a bit of bite.

For 4

4 fresh medium mackerel, whole and gutted
salt and freshly ground black pepper
zest and juice of 2 limes
1 lime, cut into chunks
5–6 tablespoons shelled pistachios (salted are fine)
1 small garlic clove
pistachio oil
olive oil

Heat the oven to 180°C/350°F/gas mark 4.

Place the mackerel in a roasting tin or large gratin dish. Sprinkle them with a little salt, pour over half the lime juice and put the chunks of lime into the cavities.

Roast for about 10–12 minutes until the skin is crisp and the flesh comes away from the backbone easily. Alternatively, cook them in a griddle pan.

Whizz the pistachios with the garlic, lime zest, remaining lime juice, a dash of pistachio oil and olive oil in a mini blender until you get a smoothish paste. Add more oil if it is too stodgy.

Season the pesto with salt and pepper and serve alongside the whole roasted fish.

SEA BASS WITH FENNEL

If you grow towering fennel plants in your garden, this is a great way to add smoky flavour to fish at end-of-summer barbecues. The fish is cooked over coals on a bed of dried fennel stalks. You could use snapper or red mullet if you prefer.

For 4

½ tablespoon fennel seeds
2 whole sea bass about 500–600g each, descaled and gutted
1 large or 2 small lemons, cut into chunks
salt and freshly ground black pepper
a couple of handfuls of fresh or dried fennel stalks

Prepare the barbecue.

Sprinkle fennel seeds over the fish and also add them, together with the lemon chunks, to the cavities. Season with salt and pepper.

Put the fennel stalks on the barbecue grill and lay the fish on top. Let them cook for 8–10 minutes on each side.

ROAST MONKFISH WITH GARLIC

Members of the anglerfish family, monkfish are rather monstrous-looking. Their body seems to consist of an enormous gaping mouth attached to a muscular tail. The tail and the liver, plus the cheeks on bigger fish, are the only edible parts. The tail flesh is firm, dense and sweet – quite similar to lobster, in fact – with the huge advantage of having no bones running through it. The French name is *lotte* or *baudroie*, and sometimes *gigot de mer* or 'the leg of lamb of the sea', thanks to the meatiness and shape of the tail.

A versatile and robust fish to cook, it is good cut into chunks and simmered slowly in wine with tomatoes, chillies and peppers, or in a curry sauce. It is also lovely in cold terrines mixed with fish that have different tastes and textures, such as salmon and sole. But my favourite (and also the fastest and simplest) way of preparing monkfish is to pot-roast a whole tail in a covered casserole with garlic and butter.

For 4

1 whole monkfish tail weighing 500–600g
3 garlic cloves, peeled and halved
80g butter
salt and freshly ground black pepper
2 tablespoons white wine vinegar

Preheat the oven to 220°C/425°/gas mark 7.

Rub the monkfish all over with garlic.

Heat the butter in an ovenproof casserole, pop in the garlic halves and brown the fish all over. Season well, then cover the casserole and put it in the oven for about 5 minutes.

Remove from the oven, add the vinegar and stir quickly with a wooden spoon. Put the lid back on and roast for a further 3–4 minutes. The fish is cooked when the flesh is opaque and comes away easily from the central cartilage.

Serve with wilted greens or the green beans recipe on page 35.

ASPARAGUS RISOTTO

This is only fast in cooking time, of course, not if you usually cook and do five other things simultaneously, because risotto needs a little technique and your undivided attention. But it's a wonderful way to put the flavour and texture of fresh green asparagus centre stage. Mix the asparagus with fresh peas, broad beans and fresh herbs thrown in at the end for a lovely springtime feast.

For 4

10–12 asparagus spears
salt and freshly ground black pepper
1.5 litres chicken or vegetable stock
2 tablespoons olive oil
1 large onion, finely chopped
250g round, risotto rice (Arborio is best)
a small glass of dry white wine
100g fresh Parmesan cheese
2–3 tablespoons mascarpone cheese

Trim off the woody ends and cook the asparagus in boiling salted water. While that is happening, bring the stock to the boil and keep it at a low simmer.

In a heavy-based pan or frying pan, heat the oil and sweat the onion for a few minutes until it has softened.

Add the rice and stir while cooking for about 3 minutes, until the grains have become partly translucent. Add the wine, stir well and let it evaporate for a couple of minutes. Then, little by little, one ladleful at a time, add the hot stock to the rice and, stirring constantly, let it soak into the grains. The rice should never swim in the stock, dry out or stick to the pan.

Drain the asparagus after about 8–10 minutes. The spears should be nice and firm. Cut off the tips, then slice the stalks. Keep them warm under some foil.

The risotto is cooked when the rice is soft right through to its heart but leaves a little bite (you may not have used all the stock). The dish should be silky smooth, thick and creamy.

There's never any harm in adding a little more creaminess, though. This is when the cheeses go in. Grate most of the Parmesan and stir it, together with the mascarpone, through the risotto, preferably off the heat. Then add the asparagus, mixing it in lightly. Season with salt and pepper and serve with a little extra Parmesan grated over at the last minute.

PASTA WITH MASCARPONE, PARMESAN & LEMON ZEST

This is another speedy dish that's perfect for when your mind is busy with things other than cooking. The lemon zest adds a subtle hint of character to the luscious creamy pasta, while making it look pretty as well.

For 2

a couple of handfuls of fresh pasta (tagliatelle or spaghetti is perfect)
2 tablespoons mascarpone cheese
2 tablespoons freshly grated Parmesan cheese
zest of 1 lemon
Fleur de sel and freshly ground black pepper

Cook the pasta until it is al dente, then drain.

Add the cheeses and lemon zest, mix well and season with salt and pepper.

Serve immediately.

GNOCCHI WITH SAGE BUTTER, LEMON & PINE NUTS

Forgive me if I'm on a bit of a citrus mission in this book, but there is something about the tangy aroma of lemons, limes and oranges that, for me, perfectly evokes spring and summer. There is always a bowl full of them in my kitchen and lately grating their zest into soups, pasta, stews and salads has become more natural than seasoning with salt. It has a lot to do with my wondrous microplane grater, discovered in Dean & DeLuca many years ago and now part of the emergency kit I take anywhere I may be called upon to do some cooking.

For 4

150g butter
a good bunch of fresh sage, leaves picked
600g fresh gnocchi
salt and freshly ground black pepper
zest of 1 large lemon
2 or 3 handfuls of pine nuts, toasted

Heat the butter in a small pan and, when it sizzles, drop the sage leaves in. Remove from the heat and let the flavours infuse.

Cook the gnocchi in a large pan of boiling salted water, removing them with a slotted spoon when they rise to the surface.

Mix the sage leaves, butter (though perhaps not *all* the butter – I use a lot as it gives the leaves room to infuse) and lemon zest into the warm gnocchi.

Add the pine nuts, season with salt and pepper and serve.

OMELETTE WITH CHERRY TOMATOES, SHIITAKE MUSHROOMS & MARIGOLD PETALS

The word 'omelette' comes originally from the French word *lamelle*, meaning 'thin strip', because of its flat shape, and gradually changed via *alumette* and then *amelette*. However, although omelettes are claimed by the French as one of their great culinary creations, you will find that everyone has an opinion, a criticism or an infallible tip to offer. Indeed, the great food writer Julia Childs took them so seriously that she considered keeping a pan solely dedicated to omelette-making a 'wise decision'. Omelettes are the ultimate in fast meals – supposedly ready in just 30 seconds – but can involve a whiff of competition and performance that I hate. It is an intensely personal thing to make an omelette for anyone, but I reckon that as long as it stays foamingly soft in the middle, yet hot enough to melt the cheese if you are using it and doesn't burn on the outside, you can give yourself a gold star.

If you feel like having this omelette, don't deprive yourself just because there are no marigolds to hand – I only added them here after an opportunistic forage in the garden! But by the same token, if you find some, perhaps they will encourage you to make this dish. They do look pretty scattered over the tomatoes and add a subtle peppery taste.

For 2

200g shiitake or oyster mushrooms
olive oil
6 eggs
50ml milk
salt and freshly ground black pepper
6 red cherry tomatoes
6 yellow cherry tomatoes
cheese (optional)
marigold petals from the garden

Fry the mushrooms in olive oil, then drain on kitchen paper and keep warm.

Whisk the eggs with the milk, then season with salt and pepper.

In a separate pan, heat some more olive oil until nice and hot, then pour in the egg mixture.

When the eggs are nearly cooked through, add the raw tomatoes and cooked mushrooms. At this stage you could add some cheese if you fancy it.

Sprinkle in the flower petals, fold the omelette over and serve.

FLAMMEKÜCHE OR TARTE FLAMBÉE

No, not a tart doused in Grand Marnier and set alight, but more a sort of thin Alsatian pizza. The *flambée* in the name comes from the ancient way of baking it near the coals of an open fire, where the fat from the bacon would flare up when it fell. You could always make your own pizza dough, or use puff pastry at a pinch, but your best bet is to buy a ready-made pizza base, perhaps rolling it out a little to make the tart nice and crispy. You could also jazz things up a bit by cutting the outside edge of the dough and plaiting it.

This may seem a lot, but for a main course serve one per person. Every bite makes you want two more. I remember the poor chefs in a tavern in Alsace years ago trying to keep up with the appetites of a ravenous pack of us after a rowdy all-night wedding party.

For 1

2 medium sweet onions
2 tablespoons oil
4–5 tablespoons crème fraîche
2–3 tablespoons soft, tangy white cheese
freshly ground black pepper
1 ready-made pizza base
150g bacon lardons

Preheat the oven to 200°C/400°F/gas mark 6.

Slice the onions thinly and sweat them in the oil until soft. Add the crème fraîche and the cheese and mix. Season with pepper.

Spread over the pizza base, sprinkle on the lardons and cook in the oven for 10–15 minutes, until the bacon is sizzling, the cream bubbling and the edges of the tart are golden.

Eat piping hot, with a salad on the side if you want to make a meal of it.

YESTERDAY'S CROISSANTS WITH MUSTARD, GRUYÈRE & LEMON

In my house, these are just as likely to be the Sunday morning croissants begging to be used up fast for a late Sunday tea after a long lunch. They make a welcome change for the usual boiled or scrambled egg brigade and will even cheer the children up on what is usually the gloomiest night of the week. It is always worth having grainy mustard and some sort of good meltable cheese in the fridge.

For 6

6 verging-on-stale croissants
25g butter
25g flour
200ml full-fat milk
75g Gruyère cheese, grated, with a little extra for the top
1 tablespoon wholegrain mustard
zest of 1 lemon
salt and freshly ground black pepper

Slice the croissants in half lengthways and toast the insides.

Melt the butter in a saucepan, then take the pan off the heat and mix in the flour to make a roux. Put the roux back on the heat and cook, stirring all the time, for a few minutes. Add the milk, using a whisk to smooth out the mixture if needs be, and bring to the boil, stirring constantly.

When the sauce is nice and thick, add the Gruyère, mustard and lemon zest, then season with salt and pepper.

Divide the mixture between the bottom halves of the toasted croissants and cover with the tops. Sprinkle over the extra Gruyère and place the croissants under a hot grill for a few minutes so the cheese melts. Serve immediately.

RACLETTE BAGUETTE

This is a popular quick teatime meal in my house when I don't have time to take the raclette contraption out and cook potatoes. It's also great for using up raclette-party leftovers.

For 4

2 fresh baguettes
olive oil
8 slices of ham
200g raclette cheese, sliced
gherkins

Heat the grill or the oven.

Cut the baguettes in half lengthways and drip a little olive oil over the cut surfaces. Lay the ham on top, then cover with the cheese. Pop them in the oven or under the grill until the cheese is bubbling.

Serve immediately with gherkins and a green salad.

SARDINES WITH BAY & ONIONS

This is a simple and aromatic way of accompanying grilled sardines, or indeed any grilled fish. Use onions from Roscoff if you can find them. Harvested in August, they keep well. They are a pretty pink colour and taste milder and sweeter than other types of onion.

For 4

70ml olive oil
2 Roscoff onions (use red onions if you can't find them), thinly sliced
2 bay leaves
4 tablespoons white wine vinegar
salt and freshly ground black pepper
8 sardines

Heat the olive oil in a saucepan and poach the onions in it for about 5 minutes. Take off the heat, add the bay leaves and vinegar, some salt and pepper, and leave to cool.

Serve warm over the grilled sardines.

GREEN BEANS WITH ANCHOVIES & OLIVES

This is a great dish to serve as a starter or with grilled steak or fish. It's equally good hot, warm or cold.

For 4

500g fine green beans
olive oil
8–10 salted anchovy fillets, rinsed, dried and chopped
1 heaped tablespoon capers
100g black olives, pitted and coarsely chopped
zest and juice of 1 lemon

Boil or steam the green beans and toss them in olive oil.

Mix the anchovies, capers, olives and lemon zest and juice together, then stir through the beans.

TOMATES À LA PROVENÇALE

In many French brasseries this is the standard vegetable, served with just about anything from steak to sole meunière. I find that invariably they soak the entire plate with tomato juices and don't always do a lot for the taste experience. I prefer eating them *telles quelles*, as a starter or as a vegetable dish on their own, but only if I have fresh parsley and thyme to hand. It's the dried stuff that gives this (and many other dishes) a bad name.

For 8

2–3 *biscottes* or 4–5 tablespoons breadcrumbs
4 tablespoons flat-leaf parsley, finely chopped
2 garlic cloves, peeled and very finely chopped
salt and freshly ground black pepper
8 medium-sized tomatoes
olive oil
1 tablespoon fresh thyme

Preheat the oven to 200°C/400°F/gas mark 6.

Crush the *biscottes* if you are using them, then mix them or the breadcrumbs with the parsley and garlic. Season with salt and pepper.

Cut the tomatoes in half and fry them for 4–5 minutes, cut side down, in a pan with some olive oil. When they are nicely caramelised, place them snugly side by side in a gratin dish and sprinkle the breadcrumb mixture, then the thyme, evenly over the top.

Bake for about 15 minutes until the breadcrumbs are toasted and golden.

CAMEMBERT

In my house, we adore Camembert and it usually gets gobbled up in one sitting. My kids even have separately wrapped triangles of it for their lunch boxes. To me, Camembert is the epitome of smelly Frenchness, and the fact that my children can't get enough of it is the proof that they have fully embraced their French food culture.

There's a disadvantage to the Camembert disappearing so quickly in my kitchen, as it is lovely to taste it over a period of a few days, experiencing the different stages of maturity and texture. Favourite ways I have of serving it to guests are roasted and molten as a starter or swathed in caramel and dried nuts and fruit. These practices are often frowned upon by my French friends – Camembert is, after all, one of the most powerful symbols of French identity. As an adored national emblem it is ferociously protected and not be tampered with! A more acceptable way of serving it is on a cheese board, where it is customary to cut out a triangle of Camembert and set it on top of the cheese. This gives guests an idea of ripeness and helps them decide to sample it or not.

This style of cheese is now made all over the world, but the true Camembert is only produced in Normandy. A genuine top quality Camembert is always made from unpasteurised milk and is carefully poured into moulds using a special ladle. A culture is added to the cheese, helping the formation of a wonderfully downy crust that we usually devour with the rest of the cheese, gladly forgetting another polite French custom of trimming it off.

Funnily enough, Camembert is one of the products that you get to prod – the aim being to feel how ripe it is before you buy your favourite. If you're not sure what you're looking for, get your *fromagier* to do it for you.

APPLES BAKED WITH CAMEMBERT

If you want to go even faster, you could always skip the peeling and hazelnut-coating part and simply bake the apples stuffed with Camembert. Either way, I like to turn the oven up high so that the apples puff up, making the end result delectably messy.

For 4

4 large cooking apples
80g melted butter
5–6 tablespoons chopped hazelnuts
1 Camembert cheese

Preheat the oven to 200°C/400°F/gas mark 6.

Peel the apples and cut a thin slice at their base to even them out if they don't stay upright. Core them, cutting out quite a large cavity. Try to keep the bottom intact so that the cheese doesn't leak out too much during cooking.

Brush the apples with the butter, then roll them in the hazelnuts, pressing the nuts into the flesh.

Cut the Camembert into chunks, with or without the rind depending on your taste. Stuff the chunks into the apple cavities, then place the apples on a baking tray and bake for about 15 minutes, until they are puffed up and the cheese is deliciously runny and melted.

Serve immediately with a nice crunchy salad.

The recipes in this chapter adhere more to a mood, a frame of mind, than to endless lists of instructions, complicated cooking or long preparation times. They include the sort of dishes you would cook when you have the afternoon, the day, or even the weekend ahead of you, but also those where methods are gentler and where one particular ingredient may be given a little more attention than usual. Here, time itself is often as important an ingredient as the edible ones, and the techniques used reflect that. Sometimes dishes need marinating, resting, slow simmering or roasting, giving each ingredient the time and space to release every last atom of taste and allowing them to mingle slowly and completely with others.

These are forgiving recipes, where strict weights and measures and exact ingredients can be tweaked and interpreted as long as the basics are respected. This is the way many of them have evolved over the centuries in France – each region takes a classic stew, roast or soup and cooks it using what's in season or readily available in the area. Thus a dish such as *la potée*, a robust country stew, finds itself with over twelve variations throughout the country. The foundations of the dish, a mix of plain and smoked pork cooked with cabbage, stay the same, whilst flavourings, vegetables, poultry, beef and veal are mixed and matched according to what each *terroir* gives up naturally.

This is where the ideas that form the Slow Food movement join slow cooking, as the traditions, countryside and culture of each area shine out through the food. These are the type of dishes served at family gatherings and village fêtes where everyone lends a hand in their preparation and enjoys the communal anticipation of the forthcoming meal. After all, this is just as important a part as the sitting down around the table and consuming of a dish. As always, the quality of ingredients used is paramount if they are to stand up to a long slow cook, although they certainly do not have to be the most luxurious; indeed the cheaper cuts of meat and offal are wonderfully tasty, and simply need a little extra coaxing and time to express their entire personality.

SLOW

BOEUF CAROTTES

This is rather a blunt title for a rich and deeply flavoured stew. As with many slow-cooked dishes, the trick is to give all the ingredients, down to the smallest chunk of celery, enough time, space and heat to give up their maximum flavour. The quantity of red wine may seem extravagant, but the almost black, sticky sauce it produces will convince you it was worth popping two corks.

For 4

10 carrots, peeled
50g butter
2 tablespoons olive or sunflower oil
1kg boiling beef
2 medium to large onions, peeled and halved
3 garlic cloves, crushed
2 sticks celery, cut into 4–5cm pieces
3 level tablespoons plain flour
1.5 litres good red wine
1 bouquet garni
salt and freshly ground black pepper
1 tablespoon tomato purée or sundried tomato paste

Chop two carrots into two or three chunks and slice the others into 5mm discs.

Melt the butter with the oil in the casserole, then add the beef and let it brown all over.

Add the onions, the garlic, the two chunky chopped carrots and the celery. Sweat for a few minutes, giving things a shake and a rough stir so that nothing burns. Sprinkle the flour over everything and stir again.

Pour in the red wine and stir thoroughly to disperse any lumps. Add the bouquet garni, a little salt and pepper and the tomato paste. Cover the casserole and cook over a very low heat or in a slow oven (150°C/300°F/gas mark 2) for about 2 hours.

Check on proceedings from time to time. If the meat seems to be drying out, add some water, stir well and return to the heat or oven.

This is a perfect dish to cook in advance, so at this stage you could let it cool right down, then put it in the fridge. The next day, heat it gently then let it boil for a good 10 minutes. Alternatively, keep on cooking, add the sliced carrots and serve 30 minutes later.

OXTAIL & CHEEK POT AU FEU

A beautifully rich and tasty version of the classic where the duo of melting cheek and tail meat work particularly well together. At my local market, there's a wonderful offal stand where I get the very cheap ingredients for my pot au feu. In France, oxtail is not the trendy gastropub staple that it has become in the UK; it's an old-fashioned dish that is all about using up every bit of the animal. Make sure you have enough leftovers for *hachis* the next day!

For 4

1 small or medium disc oxtail, trimmed and trussed by your butcher
1 ox cheek, approx. 500g
2 carrots, peeled, cut into 5cm chunks
2 celery sticks
1 leek (white part only), rinsed
2 small turnips, peeled
1 garlic clove, peeled
1 onion, studded with a few cloves
1 bay leaf
a sprig of fresh thyme
a few stalks of fresh flat-leaf parsley
salt and freshly ground black pepper
6–8 firm potatoes, peeled

Put all the ingredients apart from the potatoes into a large stock pot and cover with water. Bring to the boil and skim off any scum that forms on top, then simmer slowly for 3–4 hours, skimming again if necessary.

About 20 minutes before you want to serve, add the peeled potatoes.

When the potatoes are ready, strain the meat and vegetables. Season the broth to taste. Serve the broth first in soup bowls, then the meat and vegetables with flaky salt, *cornichons* and mustard.

NAVARIN PRINTANIER

The name *navarin* comes from the French word for turnip, *navet*, and originally it was the main vegetable used in it. My version is the best known springtime version, which highlights other juicy new vegetables as well. This dish is perfect for the first lunch of the year, when you dare to move outdoors and the air is still a bit nippy but the sun is warm. Even if you don't make it to pudding without an extra layer, you will have broken out of the dining room or kitchen at last. A simple and delicate lamb stew with young spring vegetables, *navarin* is at once light and hearty, melting and crunchy, earthy and sweet. It hails the end of winter and promises summer.

For 4

olive oil
1kg shoulder of lamb, cut into chunks
5 carrots, peeled and chopped
1 onion, chopped
1 tablespoon tomato paste
1 bouquet garni
salt and freshly ground black pepper
4 good handfuls of fresh green spring vegetables (e.g. mangetout, peas, white or purple baby turnips, asparagus, courgettes, green beans)

In a cast-iron casserole, heat the oil and brown the meat with the carrots and the onion. Pour in enough cold water to cover the meat. Stir well, scraping the bottom of the casserole to catch all the tasty goodness stuck there.

Add the tomato paste, the bouquet garni and a little salt and pepper, bring to the boil and simmer for about 45 minutes, or until the meat is tender.

Remove the meat and keep it warm. Reduce the stock a little to intensify the taste, but leave enough to ensure a nice swim for the vegetables. Put the meat back in and adjust the seasoning.

Steam the vegetables separately, keeping them nice and crunchy, then add to the *navarin* just before serving.

LA POTÉE LORRAINE

Every region of France has its own *potée*. Often different meats are mixed together – pork, duck, beef, veal, lamb – but the most important distinction is between smoked and unsmoked meats. The one from Lorraine is the most well-known. A huge hunk of a dish, this is rarely found on restaurant menus outside its region. It takes a lot of preparation and a considerable amount of time to cook, but what a lovely way to spend a chilly Saturday with friends who are staying for a winter weekend. The reward for all the effort is this great communal, flavoursome stew with the broth served as a starter, followed by plates of melting meat, sausages and vegetables.

For 4–6

2 onions, chopped
4 leeks, sliced
1 tablespoon duck fat
500g ham hock
1 medium green cabbage, roughly chopped
4 carrots, cut into chunks
2 small turnips, cut into chunks
4 garlic cloves, peeled and chopped
2 cloves
1 bay leaf
250g lean smoked bacon
4 pure pork sausages
nutmeg
6 medium potatoes, peeled and whole

FOR THE HERB CREAM
fresh herbs (e.g. parsley, chives, tarragon, chervil), finely chopped
500ml double cream
salt and freshly ground black pepper

In a large, heavy-bottomed casserole, fry the onions and leeks in the duck fat. When they are lightly coloured, place the ham on top and cover with cold water. Bring to the boil, skimming off any foam or scum, and simmer for an hour with the lid slightly to one side.

After an hour add the cabbage, carrots, turnips, garlic, cloves, bay leaf and smoked bacon. Cook for a further 1½ hours.

Finally, add the sausages, a little grated nutmeg and the potatoes and cook for another 30 minutes.

Heat the cream, add the herbs and season.

Serve the lovely ham broth in soup plates first, then the vegetables and meat with the warm herb cream.

BOEUF À LA FICELLE

This Parisian recipe first became popular in bistros in the nineteenth century. Tender beef fillet, trussed up with string, is poached in a tasty vegetable broth according to how bloody the guests like their meat. It was a favourite with my French family-in-law. It reminds me of large, boisterous family gatherings and steaming platters of vegetables being passed around the table.

Ask your butcher to truss the meat as if for roasting, leaving a length of string in order to lower it into the broth pot without burning your fingers.

For 6

1 large onion
2 cloves
2 carrots, halved
2 celery stalks
2 garlic cloves, peeled
roughly chopped fresh flat-leaf parsley
salt and freshly ground black pepper
800g–1kg prime beef fillet

Stick the cloves into the onion. Put the vegetables, garlic and parsley in a large pot and add water to a depth that will cover the beef when you come to add it. Season, bring to the boil and simmer for about 20 minutes.

Plunge the beef into the boiling stock, cover and cook for 15 minutes if you like your meat very rare, 20 for medium rare and 25 for medium.

Take the beef from the pot to a carving board, cut off the string and slice. It will be an unattractive grey on the outside but wonderfully juicy inside.

Serve with roast or sauté potatoes and horseradish or béarnaise sauce.

POULET AU VINAIGRE

Far from imparting a harsh, sour flavour, red wine vinegar gives this rich chicken stew a lovely fruity tang. Like many of France's classic chicken dishes, this one originated in Lyon. There is the usual debate about which colour vinegar to use and whether white wine should be added. I prefer to mix wine and vinegar, but have no strong feelings about the colour of the latter. As long as the quality is excellent, mix away.

For 4

120ml dry white wine
240ml good-quality red wine vinegar
110g tinned whole peeled tomatoes, chopped and drained
French mustard
1 tablespoon fresh thyme
1 tablespoon fresh tarragon, plus extra for garnish
1 free-range chicken, approx. 2kg, cut into pieces
2 tablespoons olive oil
1 tablespoon butter
3–4 medium onions, chopped
salt and freshly ground black pepper
350ml chicken stock
2 tablespoons crème fraîche

Pour the wine and vinegar into a large bowl, then add the tomatoes, mustard, thyme and tarragon.

Press the chicken into the marinade, cover and marinate in the fridge for 1–2 hours.

In a large pot warm the olive oil and butter on a medium heat. Remove the chicken from the marinade and add to the pot (reserving the marinade for later). Brown the pieces well, then add the onions and give everything a good stir.

When the onions start to become transparent, remove the chicken pieces to a platter and season with salt and pepper.

Continue to sauté the onions for about a minute, until lightly browned, then add the vinegar and the wine mixture and deglaze the pot, scraping up all the tasty brown bits.

Add the chicken stock, followed by the chicken, and give things another good stir. Bring to the boil and simmer, covered, for 20–25 minutes, until the chicken is cooked through.

You could prepare the dish up to this point a day in advance. Let everything cool down, uncovered, then chill it, covered. Reheat before proceeding with the next part.

Transfer the chicken and the onions with a slotted spoon to a heated platter and keep them warm, covered with foil. Simmer the sauce, then add the crème fraiche, stirring, for 1 minute.

Spoon the sauce over the chicken and sprinkle with the remaining tarragon.

POULET BASQUAISE

Thought to have evolved from a dish shepherds carried across the Basque hills in clay pots, this peppery chicken stew became the traditional Sunday lunch. You can vary the colours of the peppers, add the wonderful *piquillos* from the Basque country or even their Spanish cousins. But the most important ingredient remains the *piment d'Espelette*, a distinctive smoky, spicy chilli that will have you hooked. If you can't get this, do your own thing and give smoked paprika a try – it's available in good supermarkets.

For 6

1–2 tablespoons olive oil
1 free-range chicken, approx. 2kg, cut up, or 4 legs and 4 thighs
4–5 large onions, peeled and quartered
4 garlic cloves, peeled and roughly chopped
1 bay leaf
2 teaspoons fresh thyme, chopped
800g tinned whole peeled tomatoes
235ml dry white wine or water
2 red and 2 green peppers, sliced
1 large tin pitted green olives
1 teaspoon *piment d'Espelette*, plus extra to taste
salt and freshly ground black pepper

In a large soup pot warm the olive oil on a medium to high heat, then brown the chicken really well on all sides.

When the chicken is fully browned, add the onions, garlic, bay leaf, thyme, tinned tomatoes and wine or water. Cover and bring just to the boil, then reduce the heat to a simmer. Cook for about 40 minutes.

Add peppers, olives and *piment d'Espelette*, then cover and simmer for another 20–30 minutes, until the chicken is fully cooked and the sauce has thickened a bit.

Season with salt and pepper. If you refrigerate the stew overnight, it will taste even better the next day.

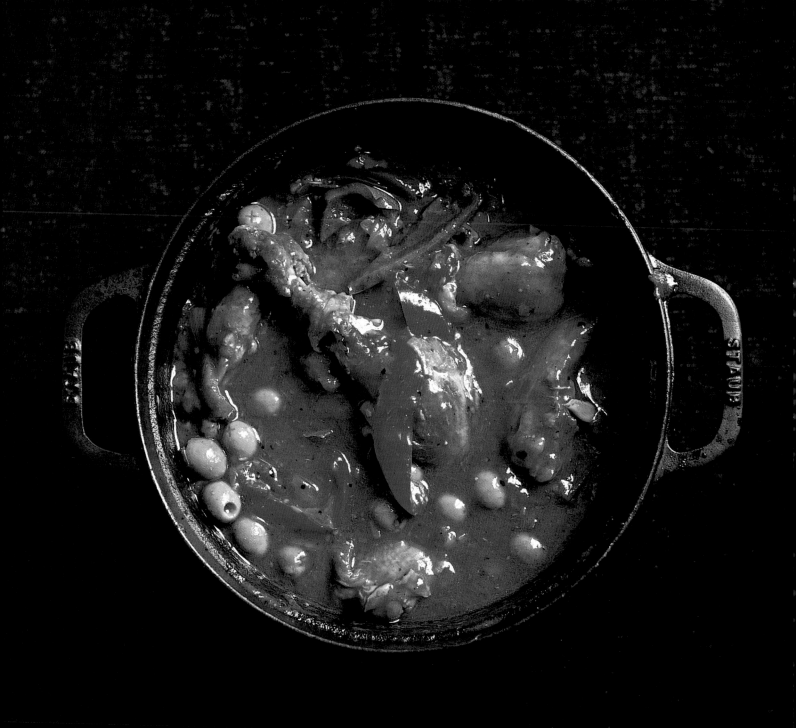

CHICKENS

The basic quality of French chickens has remained reasonable. The consumer here is used to good taste and firm bones, and fully aware of the benefits of quality labelled food. *Label rouge* is a nationwide label of quality, and a *label rouge* chicken goes beyond a free-range chicken in the UK. To qualify, chickens must be reared outside, all day long, live for 81 days minimum and eat a balanced meal of minerals, vitamins and cereals. There are strict hygiene and health checks too.

Paul and Noel Renault have been farming poultry for over twenty years on their farm in Louvigné de Bais, near Vitré. They rear chickens, pigeons and ducks with a simple philosophy – putting the birds back into their natural environment. The birds live in grassy parks, with ponds dug especially for the ducks. Paul has reintroduced rare chicken breeds such as the Coucou de Rennes, which had virtually disappeared since the 1960s. Minimum rearing time? 130 days. And everyone is fed with grain grown on the farm, pesticide-free, *bien sûr*. It's a far cry from the 'ordinary' chicken which has only six weeks to make friends in his hangar before meeting the checkout girl.

The Renaults' chickens are raised within guidelines stricter than any label. As their chickens are killed much later than a *label rouge* chicken, they are disqualified from using the prestigious sticker. This doesn't stop famous chefs supplying their Michelin-starred restaurants with Renault produce, though. The flesh is firm and tastes of hazelnuts, the bones stay hard even after a long roast or boil and their fat comes out as jelly, not water. When I'm lucky enough to get my hands on one of them, I give them a very slow pot-roast in the oven. Afterwards, the carcass will give up enough flavour for a hearty soup. But this quality comes at a price and Paul is the first to deplore it. 'When I was a boy, this chicken was anything but a luxury dish. Today, that's what it's become.'

If you want to get your hands on these fabulous chickens, go to the market in Rennes where Paul has a stand, or to one of only a few specialised butchers in Paris. Or use it as an excuse to sample the menu of some of the best restaurants across the country.

COQ AU VIN

It is such a shame that what started as the pinnacle of French cooking has become the victim of shopping centre and motorway self-service restaurants, where – it goes without saying – what is served bears little relation to the original. The dish hails from Burgundy and purists would not dream of pouring anything from outside the region into their pot, but I like to use sun-filled Châteauneuf-du-Pape. The main thing is to go for the best you can afford, avoiding 'cooking wine' at all costs. I also add a good swig of Cognac or brandy to make the taste even richer. I use *poitrine fumée* in this recipe – smoked pork belly – but chunky smoked bacon lardons would work just as well.

For 4–6

125g butter
olive oil
1 free-range chicken, approx. 2kg
2 garlic cloves, peeled, plus extra for croûtons
20 pickling onions, peeled but unpickled!
200g *poitrine fumée*, cut into chunks
Cognac
2 bottles good-quality red wine
1 bouquet garni
salt and freshly ground black pepper
250g button mushrooms
1 baguette, for croûtons

In a heavy-based casserole, heat half the butter and some oil and brown the chicken with the garlic, onions and *poitrine fumée*.

Pour the Cognac over the chicken and flame (be careful). Stir, then add the red wine and the bouquet garni. Season lightly with salt and pepper.

Bring to the boil and simmer very gently for about 3 hours, until the chicken is done.

Just before serving, fry the mushrooms in the rest of the butter until golden and add them to the casserole.

Slice the baguette, rub the slices with a cut half-clove of garlic, sprinkle some olive oil on and toast under the grill. Serve on top of the coq au vin.

NORMANDY FISH CASSEROLE

Well, a version of it. The original, *marmite Dieppoise*, comes from the coastal town of Dieppe and contains about six different sorts of fish, mussels and prawns, which are poached in cider, flavoured with Calvados and doused in cream. It's a Normandy seafood showcase in a pot. This is an altogether more modest version, using just three sorts of fish in order to make things a little easier.

For 4

1 leek, carefully rinsed and sliced
150g mushrooms
75g butter
400g salmon fillet
400g sole fillets
100g smoked hake
300ml double cream
salt and freshly ground black pepper

FOR THE (FISH) STOCK
3 or 4 fish heads (optional)
2 carrots, peeled and chopped
1 onion, stuck with a clove
1 bouquet garni
1 litre cider
300ml white wine

To make the stock, put all the ingredients in a large pot and bring to the boil. Simmer for about 30 minutes, then filter through a fine sieve.

Fry the leek and mushrooms in the butter. When they are softened but not coloured, add to the stock and simmer again for 20 minutes.

Poach the white fish in the stock for 5–10 minutes and the smoked hake for about 5 minutes until it's heated through. Add the cream, season, stir well and serve.

To make the stew more substantial, add peeled, parboiled potatoes to the stock with the mushrooms, and/or peeled halved apples with the fish.

POMMES BOULANGÈRE

This is the famous traditional potato dish that accompanies *le rosbif*. In fact it would usually cook with the beef sitting on top, benefiting from any cooking juices going. It's equally good with roast lamb, or *confit de canard*, or on its own with a few lardons scattered through the layers of potato and onions.

For 4

75g butter
olive oil
400g onions, peeled and sliced thinly
800g waxy potatoes, peeled and sliced thinly
salt and freshly ground black pepper
100ml beef stock

Preheat the oven to 200°C/400°F/gas mark 6.

Divide the butter between two separate pans. Add a little oil to each and fry the onions in one and the potatoes in the other until pale golden around the edges.

Arrange them in layers in a gratin dish, seasoning with salt and pepper as you go. Then pour over the beef stock and cook in the oven for about 40 minutes.

PISSALADIÈRE

The true *pissaladière* is an onion and anchovy tart from Nice. *Pissalat* is the ancient word for the anchovy cream spread over a bread base under a soft, thick layer of onions. Nowadays, it is more likely to be cooked on a pizza base with fresh or salted anchovies simply scattered over the top, but it is still delicious. Just be sure not to let any tomatoes spoil the experience and to have the onions as pale and slow-cooked as possible.

For 4–6

olive oil
6 onions, finely sliced
1 pizza base
12 good black olives, pitted
6 anchovies

Preheat the oven to 180°C/350°F/gas mark 4.

Heat the olive oil in a heavy-based frying pan, then add the onions and sweat until they are very soft, lightly golden and translucent.

Pile the onions on to the pizza base, making a thick layer. Scatter the black olives and anchovies over the onions.

Cook for 15–20 minutes, until the base is golden brown around the edges.

TIAN PROVENÇALE WITH ROSEMARY & OLIVES

The *tian* is a type of gratin from Provence which owes its name to the glazed earthenware dish in which it is cooked. Instead of layering the vegetables on top of each other and cooking them in eggs and cream, as in a *gratin dauphinois*, they are packed tightly, moistened with olive oil and set almost upright in the dish. Courgettes, tomatoes, aubergines, onions and garlic are the most popular vegetables used and, like its cousin ratatouille, the *tian* can be served hot, warm or cold.

For 4

4 courgettes
4 good-sized, ripe tomatoes
1 aubergine
2 garlic cloves, peeled and crushed
fresh rosemary, chopped
olive oil
salt and freshly ground black pepper
a few extra garlic cloves, unpeeled

Heat the oven to 160°C/325°F/gas mark 3.

Slice the vegetables very finely and layer them, with the crushed garlic and rosemary, alternating the colours as you go.

Sprinkle with olive oil, season with salt and pepper and scatter with the unpeeled garlic cloves.

Cook for about 40 minutes, until the vegetables are tender.

TOMATES FARCIES

The much loved and traditional family dish of stuffed tomatoes remains one of the most ubiquitous items in small French food shops. In their meat incarnation, they are sold by the *charcutier*, the butcher and the general *traîteur*, reflecting the long preparation that is required at home. Happily, they lend themselves to all sorts of interpretations. My current favourites are filled with tuna and prawn mayonnaise, which are faster – if colder! – than this, the famous main-course meal-in-a-tomato.

For 4

4 large tomatoes
1–2 tablespoons olive oil
salt and freshly ground black pepper
1 onion, chopped
1–2 garlic cloves, peeled and chopped
180g minced beef
50g black olives, pitted
1 teaspoon fresh chopped parsley
½ teaspoon fresh chopped tarragon
1 teaspoon fresh chopped chives
a few drops of lemon juice
1 egg, beaten
160g cooked rice

Preheat the oven to 180°C/350°F/gas mark 4. Slice off the top third of each tomato, making a little hat. Scoop out the seeds without puncturing the skin. Put the tomatoes in a shallow baking dish brushed with some olive oil and sprinkle with a little salt. Set aside.

In a frying pan, warm 1 teaspoon of olive oil and add the onion and garlic. Cook for 1 or 2 minutes, then add the beef, olives, herbs, lemon juice and salt and pepper. Turn off the heat, add the egg and the rice and mix everything together well.

Fill the tomatoes right up, with the stuffing coming about 2mm above the rim. Top with the tomato hats and bake for 15–20 minutes.

WALNUT SALAD WITH POACHED QUINCE

This is a fabulous autumnal combination. The quinces take quite a bit of poaching but definitely benefit from a slow soak in sweet spice-infused syrup. Try to get your hands on fresh walnuts or, if that's not possible, fresh hazelnuts. It will make such a difference to this sweet and pungent salad.

For 4

2 ripe quinces
250g mixed baby greens
a good handful of roughly chopped walnuts

FOR THE SYRUP
475ml water
100g caster sugar
juice of ½ a lemon
1 vanilla pod
all the following can be used, or a combination:
5 peppercorns
2 cloves
1 star anise
1 cinnamon stick

FOR THE VINAIGRETTE
3 tablespoons walnut oil
2 tablespoons quince syrup
1 tablespoon raspberry vinegar
a handful of fresh chopped chives
salt and freshly ground black pepper

Wash the quinces thoroughly, remove their thick skin with a vegetable peeler and set aside.

Combine the syrup ingredients in a saucepan big enough to hold the quinces comfortably. Bring to the boil, then add the quinces. Lower the heat and simmer for about 45 minutes, until they are very tender. Allow to cool in the pan.

Remove and slice each quince into 6 wedges, removing the cores, then refrigerate, covered, overnight or for up to 3 days in the syrup.

Just before serving, whisk the vinaigrette ingredients together. Add a little neutral oil if your walnut oil is too strong.

Divide the baby greens between your plates, arrange 3 wedges of drained poached quince on each plate, drizzle over the vinaigrette, then finish with the chopped walnuts.

COUSCOUS ROYAL

This dish might not be very French, but the links between France and Morocco go back a long way. One of the greatest feasts of my life was in Marrakesh, at the home of a generous and affluent fruit grower. The meal lasted over three hours and we were served dish after dish. In between the salads, pastilla, briks, brochettes, chicken with preserved lemons and, of course, couscous, there were pauses during which chilled water with rose water would be splashed on our hands by the waiters. It was heavenly. Now that harissa, flower waters and Moroccan spices are readily available, it's fun to have a go at home.

For 4 (it's a feast!)

olive oil
4 chicken legs and 4 thighs
1kg shoulder of lamb, cut into 2cm chunks
3 courgettes, cut into chunks
3 carrots, peeled and cut into chunks
200g pumpkin, peeled and cut into chunks
2 turnips, peeled and cut into chunks
4 onions, peeled and sliced
2 red peppers, sliced
5 sprigs each of fresh coriander and parsley, coarsely chopped
300ml tomato paste
2 tablespoons *ras el-hanout*
1 teaspoon turmeric
4 cloves
1 tablespoon caster sugar
1 tablespoon ground cinnamon
salt and freshly ground black pepper
100g raisins
orange flower water (optional)
100g flaked almonds
150g tinned chickpeas
4 merguez sausages
700g medium-grain couscous
harissa paste

Preheat the oven to 180°C/350°F/gas mark 4.

Heat a small amount of olive oil in a large stock pot. Brown the chicken and then the lamb on all sides. Remove from the pot, place in a baking dish and cook in the oven for 40–50 minutes. Remove from the oven and keep warm.

Meanwhile, using the same stock pot, add all the vegetables, together with the coriander, parsley, tomato paste, *ras el-hanout*, turmeric, cloves, sugar, cinnamon and some salt and pepper. Cover with water, put the lid on and bring to the boil. Reduce to a simmer and cook for 45 minutes. Soak the raisins in warm water for at least 30 minutes and up to one hour, adding a few drops of orange flower water if you like. Toast the almonds.

Drain the chickpeas and add to the vegetables, along with the merguez. Simmer for 30 minutes until everything is softened.

Tip the couscous into a heatproof bowl and pour in boiling water just to the top of the grain. Cover and let it sit for 5 minutes.

To serve, place the couscous in a mound in the middle of a large platter. Make a well in the centre of the mound for all the meat and place the vegetables and chickpeas around the mound. Sprinkle almonds and raisins over everything.

Pour the juice from the vegetables into a bowl and serve on the side. Let everyone add harissa according to their own taste.

* *Ras el-hanout* is a Moroccan spice mixture; a lovely combination that, once you have it in your larder, you will find yourself putting in all kinds of dishes. If you can't find it, replace with 1 teaspoon ground cumin, 1 teaspoon ground coriander and half a teaspoon each of ground nutmeg and cinnamon.

BUGNES

Bugnes are delicious knots of crunchy doughnut pastry, dredged in icing sugar and eaten warm. Traditionally they're eaten during Mardi Gras, a Christian festival held in February that celebrates the end of winter, preceding Ash Wednesday and the long period of abstinence of Lent. People would eat *gras* or fat to bolster their defences before forty days of eating very lightly. During this period, not only was it usual to feast on beignets or *bugnes*, but people would also dress up in costumes and celebrate the arrival of spring. Nice's Carnival is famous worldwide, but elsewhere in France Mardi Gras is mainly celebrated in schools. Every year my kids get very excited dressing up for the mini parades that are organised in their playgrounds and then spill over on to the village streets as they walk home. In our area, *crêpes* are the traditional way of using up flour, sugar and butter before Lent, but further south *bugnes* are still the favourite treat. Most famous are the twisted *bugnes lyonnaise*, though elsewhere they take on other names and shapes, from *merveilles* to *oreilles*, sometimes cut into pretty ribbons with crinkled edges, or into rings, diamonds or flat *galettes*. They are flavoured with orange flower water, rum or Cognac and always covered with lots of sugar, either caster or icing. They are very easy to make, especially if you leave out the yeast and use a food processor. Here's my quick and easy bugnes recipe:

Put 200g flour, 3 tablespoons sugar and 60g softened butter in the food processor and whiz for about 10 seconds. Add 1 tablespoon orange flower water or rum, the zest of 1 lemon and 2 eggs. Blend for another 15 seconds until a soft dough forms. Turn it on to a floured surface and roll thinly with a rolling pin. Cut the dough into strips or rectangles and fry in hot vegetable oil for about 1 or 2 minutes until golden. Remove with tongs, dredge with icing sugar and eat right away – be careful, they will stay crunchy for only a few hours!

When thinking of raw French food, the mythical bistro classic of steak tartare or Breton oysters served with malt bread and salty butter tend to come to mind. However, the increased popularity of sushi and sashimi teamed with the onslaught of molecular cuisine – a trend that looks at cooking in a more scientific way and studies the transformation of ingredients during cooking – has given all sorts of food served raw a whole new lease of life.

The French are very good at adopting a classic dish or technique and applying it to whatever takes their fancy. For raw dishes, this means that there are now carpaccios, ceviches and tartares of just about everything, sweet and savoury, from beetroot to swordfish to strawberries. Taking one ingredient and doing fifty things to it, the molecular gastronomy way, combined with greater awareness of health issues mean that vegetables are having much more attention paid to them. The result is a purer, cleaner and more subtle taste all round.

A great example is Iñaki Aizpitarte, a young Basque chef with a large reputation in France. At his Parisian restaurant, Le Châteaubriand, he serves intense centrifuged raw vegetable nectars that replace the traditional meat-based *jus*. The combination of raw and cooked, warm and cold in dishes, such as raw red cabbage in beef bouillon with herb flowers, allow texture and flavour to be packed into every mouthful.

At home, crudités remain a typical start to many French meals, the most popular mixture being grated carrots and cubes of beetroot in vinaigrette, with cucumber in cream and herbs. For my kids at school, crudités are still on the menu as starters every day. Using raw ingredients in the kitchen opens up all sorts of possibilities of playing with vinaigrettes, flavoured salts, sugars and butters, amongst the more traditional condiments. But perhaps the most wonderful aspect of doing everything in the raw is the range of colours that suddenly become available to your cooking palette.

RAW

AVOCADO SOUP

Guacamole with tortilla chips has been broadly adopted by the French as a popular aperitif to nibble on and with the onslaught of finger food, mini portions, verrines and tapas, you'll now find guacamole served in small glasses as a soup at cocktail parties, with a little dash of tequila to keep things interesting. Serve it with warmed tortillas – it is very rich, so small quantities will suffice.

For 4

1 large ripe avocado, peeled and pitted
50ml lime juice
1 medium tomato, skin and seeds removed
150ml vegetable stock
60ml double cream
salt and freshly ground black pepper
a shot of tequila
fresh coriander leaves, to garnish

Cut the avocado into large chunks, then blend all the ingredients except the salt, pepper, tequila and coriander in a mixer.

Chill in the fridge for several hours.

Just before serving, season with salt and pepper, then add the tequila and garnish with the coriander.

SORREL SOUP ON SALMON & DILL TARTARE WITH PRESERVED LEMONS

Sorrel is a wondrous *médicaliment* or medicinal food. Rich in fibre, vitamins C and E, antioxidants and omega 3, it was used in ancient times as a healing poultice and infused in medicine to treat heart, liver and stomach problems. Even the water it was boiled in was said to make the hair shiny. For some this may be part of its attraction, but frankly, I find listing so many curative properties rather unappetising and love instead to think about its lemony bite.

Sorrel can be found on market stalls from May to October. Baby leaves require no grooming, but, as with spinach, the older, tougher ones need the stalks cut right out from the heart of the leaf.

This recipe is a bit of a compromise between healthy and downright delicious, with a thick creamy soup poured over fresh raw salmon and herbs.

For 4

400g excellent salmon fillet, chopped into small cubes
1 preserved lemon, chopped finely
a handful of fresh dill, chopped very finely
salt and freshly ground black pepper
250g fresh sorrel, chopped roughly
500g potatoes, peeled and cut into cubes
double cream (optional)

Mix the salmon, preserved lemon and dill, then season with salt and pepper. Leave to one side.

Put the sorrel in a large saucepan with a splash of water and heat slowly until it has wilted and given up its juices.

Add about a litre of water and the potatoes. Simmer for 15–20 minutes until the potatoes are soft.

Whizz the soup in a blender. Season and add a little cream if you wish, although the potatoes will already make it nice and smooth.

Divide the salmon and dill tartare between four bowls and take them to the table. Pour hot sorrel soup into each bowl when you are ready to eat and it will cook the raw salmon.

CELERIAC & CARROT SOUP WITH WATERMELON & PINEAPPLE SALSA

A fresh, healthy soup packed with seasonal flavour, this can be jazzed up with all sorts of edible accessories and served in little bowls, cups or glasses, hot or cold! I have served mine with flavoured butters and pestos in the past, but for added vitamins and freshness, and to make the most of what's in season, salsas are a perfect accompaniment.

For 4

1 celeriac, approx. 500g
300g carrots
½ leek
1 litre vegetable stock
bouquet garni
50–100ml double cream (optional)
salt and freshly ground black pepper

FOR THE SALSA
300g watermelon
½ red onion
6 cherry tomatoes
200g pineapple
chives

Roughly chop the celeriac, carrots and leek.

In a saucepan, bring the stock to the boil and cook the vegetables with the bouquet garni until they are soft.

Whilst the vegetables are cooking, finely chop all the salsa ingredients and mix together well in a bowl. Leave in the fridge to let the flavours develop.

When the vegetables are soft, remove the bouquet garni and blitz in a blender until very smooth. Add the cream if you like, season with salt and pepper and stir.

Serve in warmed bowls or little cups, topped with a little salsa.

TUNA CARPACCIO WITH LIME & PASSION FRUIT

A fresh, tangy starter to serve on a hot summer evening in the garden. You need to have total confidence in your fishmonger, of course, to make sure you get the very freshest fish. It needs to be shiny and ruby red, with no smell, or at the very most a pleasant suggestion of sea air. The combination of lime and passion fruit also works well with raw scallops.

For 4

400g tuna fillet
freshly ground black pepper
2 passion fruits, insides scooped out
zest of 1 lime
olive oil
fleur de sel

Ask your fishmonger to slice the tuna extremely thinly. Alternatively, you could flatten it yourself between two slices of greaseproof paper using a rolling pin.

Set the slices on plates and chill well.

Just before serving, season each plate of tuna in this order: black pepper, passion fruit, lime zest, olive oil and *fleur de sel*.

THINGS TO DO WITH OYSTERS

Not that you absolutely have to do anything with them, of course, if they are beautifully fresh and in season. In my country kitchen, they were at the heart of the most convivial times, as several glasses of Sancerre tended to lubricate major oyster-opening manoeuvres. Just as many would be 'tasted' as finally make it to the platters. We'd rarely serve them with anything other than a squeeze of lemon, but I think it's fun to spruce them up with a bit of imagination now and then. The honey and black pepper idea is by Richard Corrigan of Lindsay House and Bentley's Oyster Bar & Grill in London – it's his favourite way of eating oysters.

For 6–12 shucked oysters

RED WINE VINEGAR & SHALLOTS

This is a good way of cutting through a milky oyster, though it is perhaps wasted on a sweet, nutty rock oyster or a Belon. Mix together 1 tablespoon very finely chopped shallot and 3 tablespoons red wine vinegar and serve next to the oyster platter.

BACON & BASIL

Fry 2 or 3 slices of streaky bacon until very crispy, then cut them into small pieces. Dislodge the oysters from their shell, but leave them in. Set a fresh basil leaf on each one, then scatter over pieces of bacon, and dribble a few drops of Worcestershire sauce on top. Serve immediately.

HONEY & BLACK PEPPER

Dislodge the oysters from their shell, but leave them in. Grind black pepper into slightly warmed clear, mild honey, then dribble a few drops on each oyster.

RADISHES WITH SMOKED BUTTER & PASTRY TWISTS

Smoked Bordier butter from St Malo has reached cult status in France in just a few short years. If you can't get it, hunt around the specialist food shops for smoked sea salt and make your own. Fresh crunchy radishes are the perfect summer lunch appetiser, substantial enough to drift into a starter. This is one of those jolly, participative dishes that always seem to help the conversation flow.

For 4

1 packet good ready-rolled puff pastry
50g butter, melted
fleur de sel
100g unsalted butter, softened
smoked salt
1 bunch of radishes, washed, topped and tailed

Preheat the oven to 180°C/350°F/gas mark 4.

Unroll the puff pastry, cut it into long strips and brush them with the melted butter.

Line a baking tray with greaseproof paper. Twist the pastry strips to form loose spirals and cook in the oven until they are golden brown. Sprinkle with *fleur de sel* and leave to cool.

Whizz the softened butter with the smoked salt in a mini food processor, then put it in the fridge to harden until you need it.

Serve the radishes with the pastry twists and the butter.

CHAMPIGNONS DE PARIS WITH FRESH HERBS & PARMESAN

Champignons de Paris are one of the mainstays of any plate of crudités. The delicate taste of fresh raw mushrooms is a lovely way to start a meal.

For 4

150g champignons de Paris
juice and zest of 1 lemon
olive oil
fresh basil or tarragon
fleur de sel and white pepper
good fresh Parmesan

Slice the mushrooms very finely and arrange them on a serving plate. Sprinkle with the lemon juice and zest and with olive oil.

Tear the herbs and scatter them over the top, then season with salt and pepper.

Finally, with a vegetable peeler, shave pieces of Parmesan over the mushrooms and serve.

ORGANIC VEGETABLES

More than ever, fresh vegetables symbolise health on a plate – especially following the food scares of recent years. Of course the French have always served vegetables as complete dishes, not simply as accompaniments to meat or fish, which is partly why they see little need to signal 'vegetarian' on restaurant menus!

Over the past few years, however, vegetable growers like Annie Bertin in Rennes or Joël Thiébault in Paris have risen in the firmament, and their produce is shipped out to three-star kitchens all over France. But Annie's pencil-thin leeks and broccoli, tender lettuce shoots and luscious herbs are not only on offer to restaurants. At the spectacular Marché des Lices in Rennes, she is behind her wooden trestle table stall, sheltered by a battered old parasol or two, twice a week from 6 am, proudly serving the locals. From time to time, she'll abandon the stand for the warmth of the café across the square, and simply leaves a scrawled note on a piece of broken crate next to the till, which says, 'Pay what you can. Please put it in this box.'

Joël Thiébault's stand at the chic organic Président Wilson market in the sixteenth arrondissement in Paris is a much more elaborate affair. A passionate botanist, he sources ancient varieties from all over the world, not just France, then grows them in his 'garden' in the countryside west of Paris. Famous Parisian chefs can always be seen stopping off at his stall, choosing from the fourteen varieties of salad leaves, six sorts of artichokes, or discovering his latest herb.

Near my house in St Germain-en-Laye, I'm lucky enough to have Joël's cousin, Stéphane, at my market. The sheer freshness and taste of many of his vegetables make things so much easier for me in the kitchen, as often I simply need to give them a bit of a wash and scrub, then serve them raw in a salad, with a drizzle of some good oil, a few drops of vinegar or a sprinkling of *fleur de sel*. Vive les legumes!

SUMMER SALAD
IN A LOAF

This is a very large and decidedly less soggy version of the wonderful *pan bagnat*, the famous fishermen's *salade niçoise* sandwich. It is a marvellous thing to bring on a picnic, being robust and easily transportable. And if you are in France your hosts will love you for providing a dish in a dish which will always match their tablecloth.

Obviously, the number of people served depends on the size of your loaf. As for the bread, if it's a day old it will be easier to empty out to make the croûtons. If it's fresh you will be more tempted to eat the crust! Vary the colours of the peppers and cherry tomatoes to make things prettier.

For 6

1 large *pain de campagne*
1 garlic clove, peeled and halved
olive oil
fleur de sel and freshly ground black pepper
3 peppers, chopped into strips
20 cherry tomatoes, cut in half
3 large ripe tomatoes, cut into chunks
a good handful of anchovies
a couple of handfuls of rocket
3 tablespoons black olives, pitted
6 sundried tomatoes in olive oil, cut into 2cm pieces
2 tablespoons white wine vinegar

Cut a disc from the top of the loaf of bread wide enough to get a large serving spoon in. Scoop out the soft bread, trying to keep the pieces intact so you will be able to cut regular croûtons of 1–2cm. Rub the inside of the loaf with one of the garlic halves.

Heat some olive oil in a large pan and fry the cubes of bread with the garlic halves, tossing regularly, until the croûtons become golden brown. Sprinkle with some *fleur de sel* and drain on some kitchen paper.

Put all the other salad ingredients in a bowl and toss with the vinegar and some more olive oil. Mix in the croûtons and spoon everything into the centre of the loaf.

If you are transporting the salad, don't add too much oil before a long journey. However, the more oil you use, the more soaked and tasty the bread will be once the salad has gone!

GOAT'S CHEESE WITH BALSAMIC CARAMEL

Roasted goat's cheese on country bread has become a real French classic. In this more delicate version, the lettuce is much less of an afterthought than it is in the original, as I love Little Gem leaves. The caramel thing is a bit of a palaver, so only attempt this if you are feeling artistic or particularly want to impress and delight your guests. It is very pretty, though, I'm sure you'll agree, and the crunchy twang of the vinegar caramel goes awfully well with the creamy cheese and fresh lettuce.

For 4

100g sugar
2 tablespoons good balsamic vinegar
4 Little Gem lettuces, leaves separated
2 little mild goat's cheeses, sliced

Place the sugar in a saucepan with 2 tablespoons of water and heat slowly. Once the sugar has dissolved, bring it to a lively bubble and leave it for about 5 minutes, without stirring, until it caramelises. It will start around the edges of the saucepan – as soon as you see this, lift the pan and swirl the syrup around to help it caramelise evenly, before placing it back on the heat again. When it's a uniform, light brown colour, remove from the heat and add the balsamic vinegar and swirl it around again. Be careful, as it will splutter and spit, and it's very hot! When it's calmed down a bit, stir the balsamic into the caramel. Put the pan back on the heat if sugar lumps form.

Leave it to cool as you are preparing the plates.

Divide the lettuce leaves between 4 plates and set the goat's cheese on top.

Once the caramel is still quite runny but hardens when you lift it in strands from the saucepan, take a wooden spoon, or a metal one if you are not very dexterous, and spin it over the lettuce and cheese. Don't worry if you make a bit of a mess the first time you try it.

Serve immediately.

CHICORY, CELERIAC, LAMB'S LETTUCE, APPLE & HAZELNUT SALAD

A very classic French salad is one with chicory, apple and walnut. For my version, there's no hard and fast list of ingredients, so feel free to play around. You could always leave something out or substitute one leaf for another. The moist crunch instantly makes you feel the benefit of the rawness of the ingredients in your mouth. Try to find fresh hazelnuts to complete the experience.

For 4

2–3 heads chicory
300g celeriac, peeled and chopped finely
3 handfuls of lamb's lettuce, washed carefully
2 green apples, peeled and sliced thinly
a good handful of shelled hazelnuts, roasted

FOR THE VINAIGRETTE
4–5 tablespoons olive oil
1 tablespoon white wine vinegar or lemon juice
salt and freshly ground black pepper

First make the vinaigrette by mixing the oil with the vinegar and seasoning with salt and pepper.

Place the other ingredients in a bowl and toss them in the vinaigrette. Serve immediately.

BLOOD ORANGE SALAD WITH RED ONIONS & BLACK PEPPER

Their magnificent colour reinforces the rawness of blood oranges, especially when they are served as here, simply sliced. Combined with red onion, they make a lively tasting starter or a gorgeous accompaniment to grilled fish or chicken. If you scrub them well, slice them very finely and leave them to macerate in their own juice overnight you can even get away with not peeling them. It is worth using that excellent bottle of extra virgin olive oil you have been saving up for something special over this salad – just a few drops will do.

For 4

4 ripe blood oranges, peeled and sliced very finely
2 medium red onions, sliced finely into rings
good olive oil
fleur de sel
freshly ground black pepper

Arrange the orange slices on a large platter, then lay onion rings over them. Drizzle olive oil over the salad and season.

Chill before serving.

DANDELION SALAD WITH SMOKED HAM, ROAST SQUASH & POMEGRANATE VINAIGRETTE

Dandelions or *pissenlits* are one of the easiest things to forage for along the sides of country roads, as long as you are sure your chosen patch has not been visited by dogs or treated with chemicals. Choose the leaves young and tender and use the flower petals for a decorative touch. In France *pissenlit* (named for its diuretic qualities) is so readily available in markets that few people would bother picking their own. This salad combines its slightly bitter taste with sweet squash, smoky ham and a tangy vinaigrette.

For 4

2 pomegranates
2 tablespoons white wine vinegar
5–6 tablespoons olive oil
salt and freshly ground black pepper
1 medium acorn squash, halved, deseeded and cut into wedges
50g butter
400g dandelion leaves, thick stems removed
100g pine nuts, toasted
6–8 thin slices good smoked cured ham

Roll the pomegranates on a flat surface, pressing down on them with your hand to loosen the seeds inside. Halve them over a bowl, squeeze out some juice, then halve again and open up the inner segments before popping the seeds out with a spoon. Drain to separate the juice and seeds. Whisk the pomegranate juice (you need 4–6 tablespoons) with the vinegar and the olive oil to make the vinaigrette. Season and reserve.

Preheat the oven to 180°C/350°F/gas mark 4.

Put the squash wedges on a baking tray, dab with butter and roast for about 25 minutes or so, until the flesh is tender and the outside is golden. Remove from the oven, sprinkle with a little salt and allow to cool.

Mix the dandelion leaves, pomegranate seeds and pine nuts in a large salad bowl. Toss with some of the vinaigrette and serve the rest on the side with the smoked ham and roasted squash.

BLACK TRUFFLES

One of my favourite places in the world is Bressac, near Périgueux in the heart of Périgord, in south-west France. It's a beautiful area, and I just love the house that I stay in when I'm there. It has a very comfortable old sofa, a big wood fire and probably the best equipped kitchen I have ever seen. There's a wonderfully seasoned, black cast iron pan that seems to cook everything brilliantly – what I would give to own that pan!

Every year I visit Bressac especially for the truffle season. Being in the right place at the right time in order to get your hands on fresh truffles, just as they come out of the earth, isn't easy to achieve. Production is small, the season is short and the harvest changes dramatically from one week to another, depending on rainfall and temperature. Truffle growers are notoriously secretive about their methods and their supplies, and the black market is lively.

Once, when on a truffle-hunting expedition with friends, a dubious farmer replanted truffles he had bought, probably from a friend or at the market, next to truffle oaks and then led his dog to the spot he had buried them! Luckily, since then, I have come to know a truffle producer with integrity, Monsieur Hugues Martin. Hugues is an agricultural engineer who decided to give up the day job and invest in fifty hectares of truffle-growing plantations in the rolling hills around Bressac. He is passionate about his land and the great treasures it hides. He keeps a trained truffle pig for the hell of it, but his star truffle hunter is an energetic little dog called Slash. When it's full season and the rain is at bay, Slash will sniff out a truffle every three or four minutes. Sometimes it might be a lesser quality *brumale*, sometimes it might not be quite ripe, or the worms might already have had a feast. But when they're good, they're very, very good, and nothing will surpass the omelette or risotto made with a truffle unearthed just hours before, and cooked in the big black cast iron pan in that well-equipped kitchen.

.D.P. Sainte-Foy de Longas. (F) 245

TRUFFE DU PERIGORD

Entière, Cat 1, Première cuiss

...le entière, origine Périgord, eau, sel

...ron 10 g de truffe, et 10 g de jus de t...

TRUFFLE SANDWICHES

This might not be the first dish that springs to mind when thinking of truffles but, short of eating them whole, it must be one of the best ways to make the most of their heady aroma and taste. It takes a little time for the flavours to flood out, so prepare yourself for a deeply truffle-infused fridge and kitchen. This is no problem for me – indeed, it's a big part of the pleasure. However, my children are as yet impervious of the delights of the fungus and roundly detest the smell, which fills the house for half of every January.

I would serve these little sandwiches as part of a meal dedicated to truffles, before something very simple like scrambled eggs or risotto – truffles really do deserve the stage to themselves.

For 4

a fresh black truffle, approx. 30g
4 slices soft white bread
50g very good salted butter, softened
fleur de sel

Slice the truffle very finely, using a mandoline or special truffle shaver.

Butter the bread and make sandwiches with the truffle slices. Wrap them tightly in cling film and leave in the fridge for two days.

Just before serving, remove the sandwiches from the fridge, unwrap them and fry them lightly in butter until they are golden on both sides.

Cut into genteel triangles, sprinkle with some *fleur de sel* and serve immediately.

TAPENADE & ANCHOÏADE

A sun-filled way to start a summer meal outdoors, with a glass of rosé de Provence or a pastis. Both these Provençal specialities are gutsy and garlicky and will have you munching your way through heaps of raw vegetables as you scoop them up before the main course. There are many versions: sometimes the anchoïade will veer towards a bagna cauda, when the olive oil is heated; sometimes the tapenade will have almonds and green olives sneaking on to its shopping list. As always, exact historical accuracy really doesn't matter, but taste does! You can treat the instructions here as a starting point. Just keep your ingredients as fresh and of as good a quality as possible, and give whatever you create a new name.

For 6

TAPENADE
250g black olives, pitted
1 garlic clove, peeled
25g capers
50g anchovies
2–3 tablespoons olive oil

ANCHOÏADE
250g anchovies in oil (if you can only find salted ones, rinse them first and omit the extra salt)
1 garlic clove
salt and freshly ground black pepper
2–3 tablespoons olive oil

Put the ingredients for each recipe (one after the other, of course!) in a mini food processor and whizz until they form a smooth paste.

Serve with raw carrots, cauliflower, peppers, tomatoes and radishes cut into finger-food sizes.

PÉRIGORD STRAWBERRIES WITH MINT SUGAR & SWEET WINE CHANTILLY

The Périgord region is famous not only for its ducks, geese and walnuts, but also for its strawberries. The light, fertile soil, stable temperatures and many hours of sunshine produce some of the best in France. The first variety to appear, in late April, is the Gariguette, a bright red, shiny, long fruit with a firm, juicy bite and fragrant taste. Springtime in a mouthful, they make it easy to resist the tasteless Spanish impostors that invade my local supermarket from the end of March. If the strawberries you find are good enough, by all means forgo the mint sugar, although it is a very pretty element of the pudding. Use a splash of sweet wine in the light syllabub, then serve the rest chilled to your guests.

For 4

400g ripe sweet strawberries
250ml whipping cream
1–2 tablespoons icing sugar
4 tablespoons granulated sugar
a dash of sweet wine: Muscat, Sauternes, Jurançon...
a good bunch of fresh mint

Wash, hull and slice the strawberries. Place them on a large platter, cover with cling film and leave in the fridge to chill.

Whip the cream with the icing sugar and some wine.

Just before serving, whizz the granulated sugar with the mint leaves in a mini blender and sprinkle over the strawberries.

WATERMELON GAZPACHO

I know this is not the most French-sounding of recipes, but it's a beautiful, healthy, refreshing soup to serve in the evening – cooling and energising after a day in the sun. I find the sweeter, milder taste of watermelon creates a good contrast with the punchy vegetables, and leaving out the usual garlic makes the whole experience decidedly kinder on the digestion!

For 4

flesh of a medium watermelon, seedless if possible
juice of 2 limes
1 cucumber, peeled and finely diced
1 red or yellow pepper (or a small version of each), finely diced
1 small red onion, finely diced
salt and freshly ground black pepper
olive oil
fresh flat-leaf parsley and coriander

Put the watermelon and lime juice in a blender and blend until very smooth.

Add the diced vegetables and chill thoroughly in the fridge, overnight if possible. You can use ice cubes to bring the temperature down more quickly if necessary.

Season to taste, then serve with a dribble of olive oil and garnished with torn fresh herbs.

Moulin
de Rimou
Farine de Blé

Blanche
Pâtisserie
type 65

Poids net
1kg

Mouture
à la meule de pierre

LA GRANDE
EPICERIE **PARIS**

QUINOA

Poids net:
500g

CARAMEL
LIQUIDE
Au Beurre Salé

Maison Vital

Galettes Fines
VÉRITABLES SABLÉS NORMANDS
Poids net 500 g

Chocolat noir au Citron et à la Bergamote

POUR CROQUER
POUR CROQUER
POUR CROQUER

dessert   Chocolat supérieur à 64% de cacao

Morilles

MENTHE
POIVREE
Mentha piperata
feuille

les jardins de Cralo
Sauce tomate
au basilic
325g

Argania
La Maison
de l'Arganier
HUILE

RIZ

Coulis
Poire

My country kitchen larder was a proper one: a narrow, north-facing room with only a tiny slit in the thick wall, covered by wire mesh to keep the mice out and let the air in. Completely lined with ceiling-high shallow shelves on one side and deep ledges on the other, it was one of my favourite places in the house. The rows of pots and packets of herbs, spices and sauces were a constantly available palette of taste with which to create new dishes. The big preserving pots filled with cherries, plums and compotes were at once a reminder of summer sun and a reassuring stock of puddings for last-minute winter meals. I also kept a considerable collection of empty jars in all shapes and sizes for homemade *confiture*. The room smelled of apples, vanilla, potatoes and candle wax. It stayed at a kind, constant temperature and always seemed to provide the answer to any culinary problem which arose in the bright, busy kitchen on the other side of the wall. I could go in, close the door, think and find the answer, even if I came out empty-handed.

But a larder doesn't need to be an entire room. A single cupboard will do, and stocking it wisely will mean you always have the basis for a good meal. A typical French larder would hold green Puy lentils for making a real soup or for serving with leftover sausages, good eggy pasta from Savoie, extra virgin olive oil and pine nuts, dried mushrooms, tomato paste and stock cubes, jars of preserved fruits, meringues and boudoir biscuits for improvised puddings, buckwheat flour for *galettes*, vanilla sugar for *crêpes*... Just knowing they are all there will make you feel a more confident cook.

The recipes in this chapter either start deep in your kitchen cupboard, or will provide the filling for those empty jam jars that you've kept. Sometimes you'll need to add an ingredient or two, but they will mainly be easy things to pick up on your way home rather than requiring a special shopping trip. They will all give you a good reason to stock up the next time you are in France and lots of ideas for when you are tempted in the French section of an *épicerie fine*, wherever that may be.

LARDER

REAL STOCK

Real stock is the starting point, the foundation of taste, for so many dishes. Keeping a stash in your freezer is at once inspirational and comforting. With these four basic versions – fish, vegetable, chicken and beef – you will never need to reach for a stock cube again.

FISH STOCK

Makes about 1.5 litres

olive oil
2 medium onions, halved
1 leek (white part only), carefully rinsed and chopped
1 celery stick
2 garlic cloves, peeled
250ml white wine
6 white peppercorns
1 bay leaf
a small sprig of fresh thyme
1.5kg white fish bones, washed
1 small lemon, sliced

In a large saucepan, heat the olive oil and sweat the onions, leek, celery and garlic until they are softened, but not browned.

Pour in the white wine and bring to the boil, stirring well. Let things simmer for about 5 minutes until you have quite a thick syrup.

Add the peppercorns, bay leaf, thyme, fish bones and lemon to the pan, cover with cold water (you'll need 2–3 litres depending on the size of your pan) and bring to the boil. Remove any scum that forms on the surface, then simmer for 20 minutes or so.

Let the stock cool and settle, then strain through a fine sieve.

If you don't want to use it immediately, the stock will keep in the fridge for 2 days. Otherwise freeze it, either in a large container or in several smaller ones.

VEGETABLE STOCK

Makes about 1.5 litres

4 carrots, cut into chunks
2 onions, chopped
2 celery sticks, chopped
1 leek (white part only), carefully rinsed and chopped
2 garlic cloves, peeled
fresh herbs (e.g. parsley, chervil, chives, basil)
6 white peppercorns
250ml white wine (optional)

Put all the vegetables into a large stock pot with the garlic, herbs and peppercorns. Add the wine, if using, then cover with cold water (you'll need 2–3 litres depending on the size of your pan) and bring to the boil. Simmer for about 20 minutes.

Let the stock cool completely, then strain through a fine sieve.

If you don't want to use it immediately, the stock will keep in the fridge for 2 days. Otherwise freeze it, either in a large container or in several smaller ones.

CHICKEN STOCK

Makes about 1.5 litres

2kg chicken bones
olive oil or goose fat
2 celery sticks, chopped
1 leek (white part only), carefully rinsed and chopped
1 onions, chopped
1 garlic clove, peeled
1 bay leaf
a sprig of fresh thyme

Preheat the oven to 190°C/375°F/gas mark 5.

Put the chicken bones in a roasting tin with some olive oil, or goose fat if you can get it, and roast for about 20 minutes, until the bones are golden and sizzling.

Remove the roasting tin from the oven and pour in 250ml water, scraping up the bits from the bottom of the tin. Put the bones and the cooking juices into a large stock pot with the vegetables, garlic and herbs and cover with cold water (you'll need 2–3 litres depending on the size of your pan).

Bring to the boil and simmer for 3–4 hours.

Strain the stock through a fine sieve. Allow to cool completely.

If you don't want to use it immediately, the stock will keep in the fridge for 2 days. Otherwise freeze it, either in a large container or in several smaller ones.

BEEF STOCK

Makes about 1.5 litres

2kg beef bones
olive oil or duck or goose fat
2 onions, chopped
2 carrots, chopped
2 celery sticks, chopped
1 garlic clove, peeled
a sprig of fresh thyme
1 bay leaf

Preheat the oven to 190°C/375°F/gas mark 5.

Put the bones in a roasting tin with some olive oil or goose or duck fat and roast for about 20 minutes, until the bones are golden and sizzling.

In a large stock pot, heat some more olive oil or fat and brown the vegetables and garlic lightly. Add the beef bones, leaving any excess fat behind in the roasting tin. Cover with cold water (you'll need 2–3 litres depending on the size of your pan).

Bring to a gentle simmer, skimming off any scum that rises to the surface. Add the thyme and the bay leaf and simmer gently for 5–6 hours, adding water if the water level gets too low and no longer covers the bones and veg.

Strain the stock through a fine sieve. Allow to cool completely.

If you don't want to use it immediately, the stock will keep in the fridge for 2 days. Otherwise freeze it, either in a large container or in several smaller ones.

VELOUTÉ DE LENTILLES DU PUY

On its own a simple warming teatime soup, but with Toulouse sausages, *confit de canard* or just a few slices of good bacon, this will make a hearty meal. Use Puy lentils, if you can find them. These little moss-green discs are the best in France, with a delicate, almost sweet flavour and a rich mineral content. The Puy lentil is grown in the Haute-Loire, not far from Lyon, where the mountains protect the lentils from too much rain. The French take their Puy lentils very seriously indeed; there is even a Brotherhood of Lentils, where you can receive a knighthood to honour great contributions to the green lentil. They are invaluable members of your larder: so much goodness packed into such a small space!

For 4

200g green Puy lentils
1 carrot, roughly chopped
1 medium onion, studded with a clove or two
a small bunch of fresh flat-leaf parsley, roughly chopped
a sprig of fresh thyme
1 small bay leaf
salt and freshly ground black pepper
150ml double cream

In a saucepan, cover the lentils with cold water and bring to the boil. As soon as the water starts to boil, take the pan off the heat and drain the lentils.

Put them back into the pan with the carrot, onion, parsley, thyme, bay leaf and a little salt and pepper. Fill with enough cold water to comfortably cover the lentils, bring to the boil and simmer gently for 25 minutes.

When they are tender, remove the thyme, the cloves and the bay leaf, pour the contents of the pan into a blender and blitz until very smooth. If the soup seems too thick, add a little water.

Add the cream, stir well and serve.

SOUPE DE POISSON, ROUILLE & CROÛTONS

Fish soup is one of those things that's perfectly acceptable to buy, not try. Indeed, just as with good *charcuterie* and fine *pâtisserie*, the French consider it a bit mad to go to all the trouble when experts have already toiled on your behalf.

But even if all you are doing to produce the soup is opening the jar, there is no need to scrimp on the accessories. This delicious starter (or main course with a salad first) deserves a perfect *rouille* and some golden cheesy croûtons.

For 4

4 garlic cloves, peeled
1 egg yolk
juice of 2 lemons
a good pinch of saffron threads
250ml olive oil, plus a little extra
200ml sunflower oil
salt and freshly ground black pepper
2 ficelles (thin baguettes) or 1 baguette
approx. 150g good Gruyère, Beaufort or, failing that, an excellent Cheddar, grated
1.5 litres good bottled fish soup

Purée the garlic in a mini food processor, then add the egg yolk, lemon juice and saffron and mix again. Then, starting very slowly, gradually pour in the oils until you have a mayonnaise texture. Season with salt and pepper.

You can, of course, make the *rouille* by hand in a pestle and mortar. It's rather tiring on your elbows, but extremely satisfying when you end up with the heady, aromatic thick cream.

To make the croûtons, heat your grill to hot and slice the bread into discs of about 1cm. Put them on a baking tray, drizzle with a little olive oil, sprinkle the grated cheese over the top and toast until the cheese is bubbling.

Warm the soup in a saucepan and serve with the *rouille* and croûtons.

POULET YASSA

Enchanted by a recent trip to Senegal, a former French colony, French friends cooked this for me and then kindly passed on the recipe. It exists in many, many versions, and is probably one of the best known dishes from Senegal.

For 4–6

6 onions, coarsely chopped
10cm piece fresh ginger, peeled and chopped
1 free-range chicken, approx. 2kg, cut into pieces
120g peanut oil
8 tablespoons lemon juice
8 tablespoons cider vinegar
1 bay leaf
4 garlic cloves
2 tablespoons Dijon mustard
1 chilli pepper (optional), deseeded and diced
cayenne pepper or paprika
salt and freshly ground black pepper
oil for frying
1 small cabbage, chopped
2 carrots, peeled and chopped
300ml chicken stock

In a large bowl, mix together the onions and ginger, then add all the other ingredients except the cabbage, carrots and stock. Cover with cling film and place in the fridge for a few hours or overnight.

Remove the chicken from the marinade, reserving it to use later. Sauté the chicken for a few minutes on each side in hot oil in a frying pan. Meanwhile, remove the onions from the marinade and sauté them in oil in a large saucepan for a few minutes. Add the rest of marinade, together with the cabbage, carrots and stock, to the saucepan. Bring to the boil and simmer for 10 minutes.

Reduce the heat to a low simmer, add the chicken, cover and cook until the chicken is done. Serve with rice.

KIDNEYS WITH MUSTARD CREAM & CELERIAC MASH

Mustard is a larder staple that goes wonderfully with liver or kidneys. The most famous French mustard is from Dijon, and is traditionally a smoother mustard that goes well with pork, veal or steak. For this dish, I would go for a wholegrain one, to give a bit of bite to the smooth kidneys. This is a hearty, cheap and robustly flavoured dish. You can replace the kidneys with liver, pork chops or beef skirt if you like.

For 4

1kg celeriac, peeled and chopped
salt and freshly ground black pepper
75g butter
6 beef, veal or lamb's kidneys, halved
olive oil
1 tablespoon wholegrain mustard
250ml double cream

Cook the celeriac in lightly salted boiling water for about 25 minutes. When it's soft, mash it with the butter, season and reserve. Steep the kidneys in cold water to clean them, then dry with some kitchen paper.

Heat a little olive oil in a pan. When it's hot, add the kidneys and cook them thoroughly over a moderate heat for around 12–15 minutes, according to how you like them.

Pour the cream into the pan, scraping the bottom of the pan to pick up all the tasty bits. Add the mustard and stir well, coating the kidneys with the sauce.

Season, serve with the celeriac mash and the creamy wholegrain mustard sauce on the side.

MUSHROOM OPEN RAVIOLI

For 4

50g butter
100g frozen mushrooms, defrosted, or a handful of dried
mushrooms, soaked
a few fresh sage leaves, torn into pieces
350ml double cream
150g mousse foie gras (optional)
8 sheets fresh pasta
salt

Here I've extended the meaning of larder to encompass my freezer because my beloved frozen food shop, Picard, does a wonderful range of mushrooms: morels, chanterelles, ceps, good old champignons de Paris and then a little *mélange* of all four. It's true that they are soggier and slimier than when fresh, but they retain a large part of their taste and require no fastidious cleaning. And they're such a useful ingredient to keep frozen – easily popped into stews and soups for extra flavour. Of course, you can use dried mushrooms in more or less the same way, give or take a bit of soaking; any well-stocked country kitchen cupboard should keep them to hand.

Melt half the butter in a frying pan to a good sizzle, then add the mushrooms and sage. Allow to colour slightly, trying to maintain the lovely shapes of the mushrooms. (If you are using dried mushrooms that you have rehydrated, this will take longer.)

Pour the cream into the pan, mix with the mushrooms and heat through.

If you are using foie gras, add it now, whisking it into the cream until it more or less dissolves.

Cook the pasta sheets in boiling water with a little salt, according to the instructions on the packet. Drain and place a sheet of cooked pasta on each plate. Put some creamy mushrooms into the centre of the pasta sheet, then lay the second sheet on top of the mushrooms. Cut from the centre to within 5cm of each corner and fold back to reveal the lovely mushroom mixture inside.

Spoon over some more creamy sauce and serve immediately.

THREE-STAR MACARONI GRATIN

In France, macaroni cheese is quite a simple affair, using up leftover bits of macaroni with some cream and a little cheese sprinkled over the top. However, this recipe isn't just any old macaroni cheese, it's Paul Bocuse's macaroni cheese. Bocuse is one of France's most colourful, revered and long-lasting (he's over eighty years old) chefs. From a family of chefs going back to the seventeenth century, he was trained by the legendary Lucas Carton and Eugénie Brazier and his restaurant, L'Auberge de Collonges, has held three Michelin stars since 1965. In his introduction to this outrageously rich version of a simple recipe – and I've left out the large black truffle he suggests! – he grudgingly concedes that the Italians invented pasta, but reminds us that even the Romans couldn't convert the Lyonnais from cream and butter to olive oil.

For 6

300g long macaroni pasta
salt and freshly ground black pepper
100g butter
50g plain flour, sifted
500ml whole milk
nutmeg
150ml double cream
150g Beaufort cheese, shaved into thin petals
a knob of butter
50g Parmesan cheese, grated

Preheat the oven to 200°C/400°F/gas mark 6.

Cook the macaroni until al dente in a large saucepan with a little salt. Drain and reserve.

While you are cooking the pasta, make a béchamel. Melt the butter in a saucepan and add the flour in one go. Stir with a wooden spoon for 1–2 minutes, then pour in the milk and season with salt, pepper and a pinch of nutmeg. Bring to the boil, stirring continuously.

Add the cream and most of the Beaufort to the béchamel and continue to cook, stirring gently until the cheese has melted.

Grease a gratin dish with butter. Add a layer of macaroni, followed by a layer of cheese sauce and alternate in this way till the dish is full, ending with a layer of sauce. Spread the rest of the Beaufort over the top and sprinkle with the Parmesan.

Bake in the oven for about 15 minutes, until it's nice and golden.

LUXURY THREE LAYER PARMENTIER

This type of French shepherd's pie is traditionally a dish for using up leftover beef and vegetables from the poached meat stew, pot au feu. However, its versatility and practicality make it a great base from which to play around with layers and ingredients. You can vary them to your heart's content. Here I'm using tinned confit of duck – another favourite larder staple.

For 6–8

6 legs of confit of duck
25g butter
olive oil
2 shallots, finely chopped
1 garlic clove, finely chopped
220g wild mushrooms
500g potatoes, peeled, boiled and mashed
500g sweet potatoes, peeled, boiled and mashed

Heat the duck legs, together with their fat, gently in a saucepan. Remove from the fat and pull the meat apart, keeping the pieces fairly chunky and substantial. Reserve.

Melt the butter and a little oil in a heavy-based frying pan. Sweat the shallots and garlic but do not colour.

Add the mushrooms to the pan and lightly fry until they are golden and slightly crispy. Reserve until required for the topping.

In a large gratin dish build up the layers, starting with duck, followed by mashed and sweet potato, and ending with the mushroom mixture.

You can serve this immediately if all the ingredients are nice and warm. Alternatively, cover lightly with foil and reheat later in a warm oven.

SEL DE GUÉRANDE

For centuries, the marshes around the beautiful medieval, fortified Breton town of Guérande have produced high-quality natural salt, moist and packed with minerals. The town is surrounded by salt plains, which have the added bonus of being fabulous nature reserves; a great patchwork of still water pools that creates a natural haven for the most amazing birdlife.

There are two types of salt produced in Guérande and similar places around France. *Gros sel* is unrefined, grey in colour and is imparted by the clay of the salt pools. It has a lovely seaweedy taste and is much lower in sodium than refined salt. My designer salt cellar at home has long since been exchanged for a hearty-looking preserving jar filled with wet, irregular crystals of *gros sel Guérandais*. It is a simple and pretty much compulsory condiment for dishes such as beef *pot au feu*, or *potée*, where its strong crunch livens up the melting meat and vegetables. Somehow this salt doesn't seem such an unhealthy thing to be adding to my cooking; it holds no chemicals or preservatives and it gives personality to each mouthful of food.

The crème de la crème of salt, however, is *fleur de sel*. Harvested from the surface of the salt pools, where it forms a crust, it has recently become extremely trendy in France. With raw fish and vegetable dishes being served more and more often, some *fleur de sel* and a little lemon or lime juice provide both a condiment and a cooking method. Little bowls of *fleur de sel* of all colours will greet you in restaurants or at food-fashion-conscious friends' tables.

In Guérande, the fleur de sel has a marvellously delicate taste of violet, a moist filo pastry texture and, somehow, feels less salty than salt. Its refined nature makes it the perfect *exhausseur de goût*, taste booster, in both savoury and sweet dishes. Yes, I did say sweet dishes! Pierre Hermé, the world-famous French *pâtissier*, insists that 'the most important element for sugar is salt'. All through his cakes, chocolates, macaroons and toffees, you will come upon the slightest hint of *fleur de sel*. A salt crystal in a piece of cake or a buttery biscuit will give it texture – you will feel it in your mouth before it melts away, adding an extra dimension to the food. I never use *sel fine de table* any more, all my salt needs are being met by the delightful, delicate salts from Guérande.

GALETTES DE SARRASIN OU BLÉ NOIR

These are the rustic-looking *crêpes* your eggs, ham and cheese come wrapped in when you order from the savoury side of a Breton *crêperie's* menu. The grey, grainy buckwheat flour gives a rougher texture and slightly tart taste, contrasting beautifully with the smooth, white, plain flour of the pudding version. It's very important to let the batter rest overnight, so the starch swells and makes for a lighter, smoother-flowing mixture.

For 6

3 eggs
350ml water
150g buckwheat flour
salt and freshly ground black pepper

Beat the eggs and water together very well in a large mixing bowl.

Sift the flour, salt and pepper, then add to the egg mixture.

Mix together, cover with cling film and refrigerate overnight.

To cook, heat a large non-stick pan over medium heat. When the pan is hot, pour 60g of batter in the centre, then tilt the pan around so that it spreads out thinly.

Cook until lightly browned, about 2 minutes, flip and cook for a further minute.

Keep the galettes warm as you go, unless you are feeding them to your guests one by one!

RED ONION JAM

Red onions are such kind kitchen companions, with their sweetness and their beautiful colour. They add taste without harshness to coleslaw and salads when raw and, though they require spices and a little wine or vinegar when cooked, they provide a gentle base for stews and soups. In France they are in season from June right through to March, so you have plenty of time to stock up your larder with chutneys and savoury jams. This versatile recipe is great with grilled meat and fish, as a cushion for little goat's cheese tartlets or simply as a condiment with good cheese.

For 5–6 jam pots

300g sultanas
150ml olive oil
2kg red onions, sliced
300g sugar
600ml red wine
6 tablespoons balsamic vinegar
6 tablespoons crème de cassis
salt and freshly ground black pepper

Cover the sultanas with warm water in a bowl and leave to soak for 30–40 minutes.

Heat the olive oil in a large pan and sweat the onions for 10–15 minutes, until they are soft, then add the sugar. Stir well and cook until they are melting and caramelised.

Drain the sultanas and add them, together with the wine, the vinegar and the *crème de cassis*. Let it all cook for 25–30 minutes, until the liquid has been absorbed or evaporated and the jam is thick and sticky.

Season with salt and pepper, transfer to clean, dry pots, put the lids on and turn them upside down immediately.

Leave to cool and store them away.

PICKLED CHERRIES

Although, on the whole, the French are not madly into pickles and chutneys, this is perhaps their most popular savoury preserve. It is very good with a great slab of chunky, rustic pork terrine, cold beef or ham, but best with a smooth and tasty duck or goose liver pâté. As with my jam recipes, when I say 'pots' I mean the ones you have kept and washed from your morning marmalade or *confiture*.

For 4 or 5 jam pots

2kg ripe red cherries
4–5 tablespoons soft brown sugar
1.5 litres white wine vinegar
8 black peppercorns
3 juniper berries
1 bay leaf
2 cloves
salt

Wash and dry the cherries, leaving about 5mm of stalks still attached. Divide them between the clean, dry pots and sprinkle the sugar over them.

Bring 1 litre of the vinegar to the boil with the peppercorns, juniper berries, bay leaf, cloves and a little salt. Boil for 5 minutes.

Cool, then pour over the cherries and leave them to marinate for 24 hours.

Next day, strain the marinade from the cherries into a saucepan, add the rest of the vinegar and boil again for 10 minutes.

Pour over the cherries, filling the pots right up. Screw on the lids tightly and turn the pots over, leaving them to cool completely before you store them away.

Leave for at least a month before opening.

WALNUT TARTE

Most of my French girlfriends will have a nutty tart in their recipe collection, either a sticky, pecanny sweet pie, or something drier and fluffier, like this one, involving ground almonds. It's a love affair between coffee and walnuts; great with tea and coffee, or slightly more sophisticated, as a dessert. Of all the nuts, walnuts are the ones that are usually found in my larder – they keep for ages.

For 8–10

250g plain shortcrust pastry
130g butter
100g caster sugar
3 eggs
100g plain flour, sifted
50g ground almonds
140g walnuts, roughly chopped
10 walnut halves

Preheat the oven to 180°C/350°F/gas mark 4.

Roll out the pastry thinly and line a 22cm flan ring with a removable base. Trim off any excess pastry. Put the lined tin in the fridge while you are making the filling.

In a bowl, cream the butter and sugar together with a hand-held blender until smooth.

Beat in the eggs one by one, then spoon in the flour and ground almonds. Mix well.

Add the chopped walnuts and mix through.

Remove the flan ring from the fridge and pour in the walnut mixture, then top with the walnut halves.

Bake in the oven for about 20 minutes, until the top is a light golden colour. To check if the centre is cooked, slip a skewer or sharp knife into the centre. It should come out clean.
Allow to cool and then remove the ring before serving.

PETITS SUISSES WITH PINK PEPPERCORN SUGAR

A petit suisse is probably the first dessert any French baby will try. They're mini cylinders of creamy goodness wrapped in paper. Even for grownups, they're a great thing. If petits suisses aren't the usual pots that fill your fridge shelf, then any good plain *fromage blanc* or yogurt will do. Vanilla, instant coffee, cinnamon, nutmeg, fresh mint, mild pepper... there are lots of ways of waking up the plain base of a petit suisse. I've chosen a flavoured sugar, as this is all the rage in France at the moment. It has the added advantage of being extremely pretty, too. If you have a few strawberries to hand, they would be a welcome addition.

For 4

1 level tablespoon pink peppercorns
3–4 tablespoons granulated sugar
4 plain petits suisses

Whizz the peppercorns and the sugar in a mini blender.

Just before serving, turn the petits suisses on to individual plates and sprinkle some pink sugar over them.

BABA AU RHUM

Rum babas are little sponge cakes soaked with rum. Normally you would buy these in in a good *épicerie fine* or make them at home, but I am quite fond of the jarred ones – the cake to rum ratio of the jarred variety is very much in favour of the rum. So I always have a jar of them in my larder. They're easy to serve, one or two per person, they stay lovely and moist as they've been soaking in the jar for a while. This recipe for dolling up the little jars of rum-sodden babas is a very useful cheats' pudding device.

For 6

1 jar rum babas (usually in rum and vanilla-flavoured syrup)
some good brown rum
200ml whipping cream

Turn the contents of the jar out into a mixing bowl. Add brown rum to taste (about 3 tablespoonfuls in my case), stir and leave to rest.

Whip up the cream until it's firm.

Distribute the babas between 6 pretty glasses, pouring the syrup around them as you go.

Top with whipped cream and add a straw to drink up the rum syrup below.

MADELEINES

Thanks to Marcel Proust, who mentions the little cakes in his novel *À la Recherche du Temps Perdu*, madeleines are the most iconic of French teatime cakes. They are wonderful to bake on a rainy afternoon with the kids. In France there has recently been a craze for playing around with the recipe, with all sorts of savoury and spicy creations appearing, from green tea to spinach and ricotta. This is one time when I am firmly on the side of tradition and stick as near as possible (with thanks to famous chef Guy Savoy) to the famous buttery madeleine de Commercy I first tasted in a Paris bakery many moons ago.

Makes about 16

500ml whole milk
5 large eggs
200g sugar
200g plain flour, sifted
1 level teaspoon baking powder
120g salted butter

Preheat the oven to 200°C/400°F/gas mark 6.

Put the milk, eggs and sugar in a saucepan and heat while whisking vigorously for a few seconds until the custard mixture mousses up. Take it off the heat and cool, whisking constantly.

When completely cold, add the flour and baking powder and mix with a wooden spoon. Melt the butter and add little by little. Leave to rest for about 10 minutes.

Use a silicone baking mat, or grease the ridges of a madeleine tin with extra butter using a pastry brush. Fill the moulds not quite to the top and then cook for about 10 minutes, until they are puffed up and golden.

Remove from the oven, take them out of the mould immediately and leave to cool. They won't last long!

LANGUES DE CHAT

Langues de chat are a sort of French equivalent of the ice-cream wafer. The recipe is a handy one to master, if only to claim some input when you serve shop-bought ice creams or bordering-on-boring fruit salads.

Makes about 20

115g butter, softened
115g granulated sugar
2 medium or large eggs
100g plain flour
1 vanilla pod

Preheat the oven to 200°C/400°F/gas mark 6.

With electric beaters, beat the butter with the sugar until pale and fluffy, then add the eggs one by one, beating all the time.

Sift in the flour at the end and mix with a wooden spoon or spatula until smooth.

Split the vanilla pod in half, scrape out the seeds and stir them into the mixture.

Place a silicone baking mat or baking parchment on a baking tray.

Put the biscuit mixture into a pastry bag (a freezer bag cut at the corner will do just as well) and squeeze tongue shapes about 5cm long on to the baking tray about 3cm apart.

Cook for 5–6 minutes, until the biscuits are golden around the edges but still quite pale in the centre.

Remove from the baking tray and cool on a wire rack.

VANILLA

The French love vanilla – it's part of all sorts of dishes, from crème caramel to flan, from milk and cream puddings and *îles flottantes* to *crème anglaise*. Other spices, associated with Indian and Asian cooking, have allowed it to turn up in savoury dishes as well; teamed with cumin and saffron, for instance, vanilla is often served with seafood. I once visited the wonderful Réunion Island, off the coast of Madagascar, where vanilla is grown. I sampled a recipe for vanilla duck that seemed to use masses of pods – the result a delicious gunge of slow-roasted duck on a pile of onions smothered in vanilla sauce. Once it's left its country of origin, vanilla has to be used more sparingly than that – it's an expensive ingredient, precious even, like a sweet truffle.

The two best known varieties are Bourbon vanilla, mostly grown in Madagascar, and Tahitian vanilla, a fat, dark pod from Polynesia. The latter is judged to have the better aroma of the two, and is priced accordingly. But despite the cost, vanilla must still be a cornerstone in your larder. There are some reasonable vanilla extracts in the shops, but most are pretty bitter or weak tasting, and even if our nostalgic palates like to recognise the taste of dozens of vanilla sponges from our childhoods, it is time to retrain them to accept pods or nothing!

In my country kitchen, I used to be lucky enough to have a constant supply of fresh, moist, shiny, fat vanilla pods, destined for the professionals and sold in vac packs of twenty. It was marvellous, and I would gear many meals to my fortunate larder contents. Very often my puddings were simply fresh-from-the-churn vanilla ice cream with home-made caramel sauce. Who dared first use 'vanilla' to mean 'plain'? There is something magical about the airy creaminess of freshly made vanilla ice cream. Now my supply has dried up, I am much more sparing when using vanilla, and try to be careful about how I keep the two or three pods that I always have on hand. The popular way of storing vanilla is in sugar, thus flavouring it. But I find this tends to dry the pods out too quickly, and I prefer to wrap mine tightly in cling film and pop them in a sealed bag in the door of my fridge or in a cool cupboard until I'm ready to use one.

TRUFFES AU CHOCOLAT

What better way to spoil your guests right at the end of the meal? These are a far cry from my first experience of a chocolate truffle – an ultrasweet, supposedly champagne-flavoured supermarket one. I've played around with the outside, rather than the inside, to vary the flavours and the colours.

Try to find the best chocolate you can. High and pure cocoa-butter content, rather than high cocoa-solids content, is the way to go. The cocoa butter means the chocolate has a good base of flavour, will be smooth on the palate and easy to melt.

For 6–8

450g good-quality chocolate (*couverture* if you can get it)
250ml double cream
1 tablespoon cocoa powder
1 tablespoon icing sugar
1 tablespoon powdered *piment d'Espelette*
1 tablespoon powdered pistachio nuts (unsalted shelled pistachio nuts blitzed to a powder)

Break the chocolate into small pieces and put them into a large heatproof bowl.

Bring the cream to the boil and pour into the chocolate. Mix together gently until smooth and allow to cool.

Prepare four separate plates with the powders.

When the truffle mixture has cooled right down and hardened, scoop out small amounts with a spoon and roll in the palms of your hands to form little balls. The heat from your hands will make the surface a little sticky, which is perfect for rolling the truffles in their coatings.

Roll in the powder of your choice and allow to cool further.

Leave the truffles in a cool place until you wish to serve them. It is best not to use the fridge, as they may soak up the moisture, thus spoiling the effect of the powders.

THE BEST APRICOT JAM

This has to be one of the most satisfying and comforting activities in a country kitchen, making the most of the abundance of seasonal fruit, covering every surface expectantly with jars and sugar, thinking ahead to cooler teatimes around the fire with the fruits of your summer's labour. The hardest part of making jam, I find, is the careful preparation of the fruit. This is why apricot jam is my lazy favourite. They are easy to check for bruises, require no pampering and the stones come away from the flesh easily. This recipe lets the fruit cook on its own with the sugar. I don't use a thermometer and the results have always been spot on.

For 10–12 jam pots

3kg apricots, not too ripe
3 vanilla pods, split in half lengthways
2.5kg caster sugar
juice of 1 lemon

Rinse the apricots, then cut them in half and remove the stones. Cut the halved vanilla pods into small pieces of about 1cm long.

Put the apricots in a very large stainless steel or copper pan. Add the sugar, lemon juice and vanilla and stir very well. Leave to rest until the sugar has completely dissolved and the vanilla has spread its flavour throughout the fruit. Leave overnight if you like.

Bring the pan to the boil and boil vigorously for 5 minutes, stirring constantly. Test the jam by cooling a plate in the fridge well before you start cooking, then dropping a small amount on the cool surface. If the jam puckers and a skin has formed when you push your finger though it, it's ready. Don't worry too much about this, though. I find the 5-minute-boil rule does the job wonderfully.

Pour the jam into clean, dry jam jars, filling them right to the top. Screw the tops on tightly and immediately turn the pots over on to the lids. Leave to cool before storing in a dark place.

CONFITURE DE VIEUX GARÇON

This is more of a ritual than a recipe. *Vieux garçon* means hardened bachelor, and this is a dish to warm the cockles of a lonely heart over the winter months. It is simply layers of fruit macerated in alcohol. The trick is to make it in the tallest, most beautiful jar you can find. The fruit needs to be unbruised and carefully prepared – topped and tailed – as for jam. Use eau de vie, Cognac or any fruit-based alcohol. As the seasons pass, add layers of fruit and a good splash of alcohol. There's no need to stir.

I remember my dear friend Louisette standing in her tiny kitchen in the Vendée, at intervals throughout the summer months, plonking handfuls of cherries, raspberries, strawberries and small yellow-green plums or *mirabelles* into an enormous glass jar with a little tap at its base, then topping up with Armagnac and replacing the wide cork. When late summer evenings were a bit chilly, we would have a sneak preview and pour ourselves a little glass of the fruity nectar to drink with coffee.

Even if I use the word 'posh' with tongue firmly in cheek, there are always times when a little pomp and circumstance are necessary when you are entertaining. The French definition of what is or isn't 'posh' has swung around regularly through the decades. The fall from grace of the event previously known as the dinner party has also occurred there over the past ten years. When I first arrived in the eighties, my French friends would imitate the formula so well learned from their parents: a quickish drink with light nibbles before a full *entrée, plat, fromage* and *dessert*, then back to the sofas for coffee. Within my *belle famille*, table seatings followed strict etiquette, with my grandfather-in-law as the pivotal point, always in the prime, middle seat, befitting his age. Once his eldest daughter (my mother-in-law) was seated on his right and his eldest daughter-in-law on his left, the husbands and lesser females could alternate down according to age, until they reached the mere girlfriend of the second youngest grandson (me) right on the edge of the table. Once we were married we enjoyed the traditional special newlyweds' favour of being sat next to each other until our first anniversary, but still often found ourselves on the fold-away stools. Even amongst my new French friends the same sort of rules seemed to be religiously kept, from serving wine to cutting cheese on the cheeseboard, and though I found it fascinating, it did all seem rather stiff.

Nowadays things have lightened up significantly, with courses skipped whilst entertaining in the kitchen, or three-hour aperitifs being served around low tables in the sitting room. The dining room seems to have become semi-obsolete.

But making meals a little more special doesn't have to depend on using your best china or following intricate etiquette. It doesn't mean long and complicated cheffy recipes. You are in your home, not a restaurant. Making things a little more sophisticated has much more to do with thinking through a meal more carefully, playing with presentation of the food, and finding new and interesting ingredients.

POSH

VICHYSSOISE

This famous and much loved French soup is a rather formal but tasty starter whose ingredients can be picked up fresh from the market all year round. If you announce to a French greengrocer that you are making stock, he will put together a collection of vegetables for you. As leeks are so flavoursome, you could save yourself the trouble of making your own stock and just use water and leeks for this recipe. But it's hard not to be tempted when you're faced with the choice, quality and facility of today's vegetable market stand. I quite like my Vichyssoise warm so that's what I am suggesting in this recipe, though it is traditionally served chilled. If you like it cold, replace the butter with olive oil when you sweat the leeks.

For 4

50g butter
2 leeks, thoroughly rinsed and chopped
300g potatoes, peeled and chopped
1 litre vegetable stock
salt and freshly ground black pepper
double cream (optional)
chopped fresh chervil, tarragon and/or parsley

Heat the butter in a saucepan and sweat the leeks without colouring. Add the potatoes, give things a good stir and cook for several minutes.

Pour in the stock and bring to the boil. Leave to simmer for about 10 minutes, until the vegetables are soft.

Blitz in a blender, season with salt and pepper and add more stock or water if the soup seems too thick.

You could add a little cream if you like before serving, garnished with the fresh herbs.

LAMB'S LIVER WITH TOMATOES, BEETROOT & PARSLEY

For 4

1 lemon
olive oil
2 tablespoons chopped fresh flat-leaf parsley
fleur de sel and freshly ground black pepper
20 cherry tomatoes of different types and colours, halved
200g mini beetroot, cooked and halved or sliced
400g lamb's liver, sliced

Mix the juice from the lemon with a little olive oil, add the parsley and season with *fleur de sel* and pepper.

Arrange the tomatoes and the beets on the plates and drizzle with the vinaigrette.

Heat olive oil in a frying pan and fry the liver until it is crispy on the outside and pink inside.

Season with *fleur de sel* and pepper and serve immediately on the tomatoes and beetroot.

In France, liver is traditionally served to kids as it's so good for you – the same still happens with sheep's brains and cod's liver. Probably not considered the most delicious things in the UK, there isn't quite as much squeamishness towards these dishes in France. For this dish, both calf's and lamb's liver are equally suitable and delicious; I've chosen lamb's as it will have a slightly milder taste to it.

DECONSTRUCTED BLANQUETTE DE VEAU

A grand classic, revisited here as a nod to the deconstruction craze, where elements of a dish are dismantled and served separately. In its traditional form, it's a rich casserole with chunks of meat and carrot in a white creamy sauce. To have a bit more fun, and to provide abundant amounts of creamy sauce for everyone, you can try serving it in individual, layered portions in mini cast iron casserole dishes that have become all the rage both in France and the UK. Whichever way you choose, serve with fluffy white rice to soak up the sauce.

For 4

1kg pieces of shoulder and belly of veal
1 leek (white part only), carefully rinsed
1 celery stick, cut into 10cm pieces
3 carrots, peeled and cut into chunks
2 onions, peeled
salt and freshly ground black pepper
150g button mushrooms, finely sliced
80g butter
200g rice
1 heaped tablespoon plain flour
200ml double cream

Put the meat and all the vegetables apart from the mushrooms in a large, heavy-based casserole and fill with cold water. Add some salt and pepper, bring slowly to the boil and skim off any scum that forms on the surface, then leave to simmer for about 1½ hours.

Remove the meat, cut it into bite-sized pieces and keep it warm.

Pour the stock through a fine sieve and set aside the carrots but discard the rest of the stock ingredients. Slice the cooked carrots and keep them warm.

Fry the mushrooms in 30g of butter until they are golden and crispy.

Cook the rice, rinse it and keep it warm.

Simmer the stock until it is reduced by about a third.

Melt 50g of butter in a saucepan over a low heat, add the flour and cook for a few minutes before pouring in some of the stock. Whisk until smooth and then add the rest of the stock, stirring all the time to make the sauce smooth and thick. Finally, stir in the cream, heat through and season to taste.

At this stage, you can simply reunite all the ingredients and serve in the casserole with the hot rice, or make layers of rice, carrot, meat and mushrooms in individual mini casseroles and serve the sauce on the side.

FRENCH BREAD

The baguette is perhaps the most famous of French symbols, an enduring icon of the best of French food. A few years ago, the true quality of its pale caramel crust, creamy irregular inside and characteristic nutty moist taste was seriously threatened by the spread of industrial production. It seemed that great, pale, spongy, tasteless *pain* and baguettes had invaded the country's bakeries. The counter-attack came from a handful of passionate artisan bakers, led by famous *boulangers* Lionel Poilâne and Jean-Luc Poujauran in Paris, who championed traditional techniques and had half of Paris queuing again for the best bread in France.

I have always been fascinated by how patiently and neatly the French will wait in line for their daily bread. Fresh crusty bread once, or even twice a day is such a far cry from the soft white loaves or the sweet wheaten bread I ate (and still love) growing up in Ireland – the kind that would keep for days. But now I am lucky enough to have a marvellous bakery, open from seven till seven every day but Sunday, just fifty metres from my home. At last I find myself adopting the French habit of fresh morning baguette, if only to make sure the children have a good breakfast. Queuing at Chez Laurent in the evening before dinner, I've noticed the lengths some people go to in order to maximise the freshness of their sacred baguette. They will order and pay for it before doing the rest of their food shopping, come back about an hour later, skip the queue (never a problem!) and pick up the freshest possible bread with simply a nod to the baker's wife.

Although the amount of bread the French eat is diminishing, they still consume it at each meal and at each course, with the exception of soup. But even then it sneaks in as crunchy croûtons in a fair few recipes. It is more and more common to see specialised breads made with dried fruit and nuts served with the cheese course. *Fougasse*, a bread made with olive oil and studded with bacon lardons, olives or herbs, is now extremely popular all over the country, often nibbled on with tapenade at aperitif time. The pretty loaf in the picture comes from a specialised baker at Rennes market, who produces his loaves using recipes from the twelfth and thirteenth centuries. His stand is easily spotted thanks to the long queue stretching through the covered hall. Beautiful.

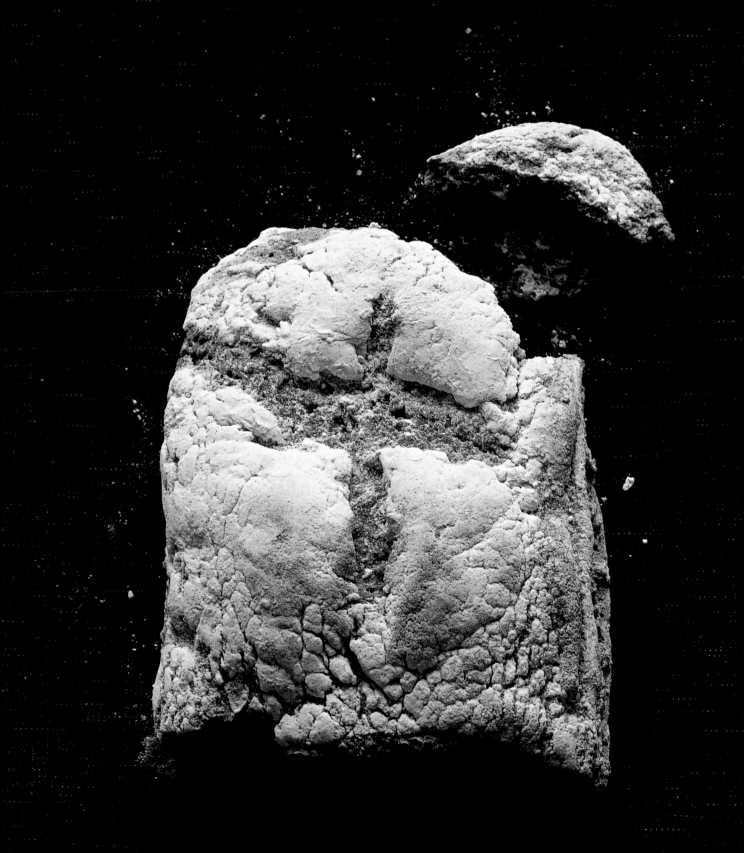

POULE AU POT

As rich and decadent as it is simple to prepare, this great French classic is similar in method to blanquette de veau (see page 130) where you cook the meat in a tasty stock and then finish the sauce with cream and butter. Traditionally it is made with a fully grown *poule*, rather than a younger, more tender *poulet*, and nowadays you must choose your bird wisely. One of Paul Renault's Poulet de Bresse or Géline de Touraine chickens (see page 55), both of which are reared for over a hundred days, would be perfect for this lovely, wholesome country dish.

For 6–8

1 free-range chicken, approx. 2kg
2 onions, peeled and sliced
2 carrots, peeled and cut into large, even-sized pieces
1 leek, thoroughly rinsed and cut into chunks
1 celery stalk, chopped
½ turnip, cut into pieces roughly the same size as the carrots
1 bouquet garni
500ml double cream
25g butter (optional)
25g flour (optional)
salt and and freshly ground white pepper
125g cooked long-grain rice per person

Put the chicken in a large saucepan, then cover with cold water and add all the chopped vegetables and the bouquet garni. Put on the lid and bring things to a gentle boil. Cook for about 2 hours, topping up with boiling water if necessary. The vegetables should hold their shape.

When the chicken is nicely poached, remove it from the pan and carve into pieces. Reserve and keep warm.

Strain the cooking liquid, keeping the vegetables and discarding the bouquet garni.

Put the stock back into the saucepan, bring gently to the boil and reduce for about 10–15 minutes to intensify the flavour. Add the cream.

If you prefer a thicker sauce, make a roux by melting the butter in a saucepan, adding the flour and cooking over a gentle heat for a few minutes until the flour and butter make a paste. Remove from the heat and add some hot stock, whisking all the time. Pour the thickened sauce into the main saucepan and heat gently, stirring all the time so no lumps form.

Season and serve the sauce poured over the chicken, vegetables and hot rice.

RETRO QUAIL ON TOAST WITH FOIE GRAS & HOT GREEN GRAPES

Cailles farcies or stuffed quail was such a big dinner party favourite in 1970s France; it's one of those chi-chi dishes many people associate with French restaurant cooking... outside France. It's here in a slightly tongue-in-cheek capacity, which doesn't stop it from being classic and delicious.

For 4

4 nice plump quail
2 tablespoons olive oil
25–30 green seedless grapes, halved
a knob of butter
4 thick slices brioche, toasted
4 slices terrine de foie gras, *mi-cuit* if you can find it

FOR THE STUFFING
25g butter
2 shallots, finely chopped
2 tablespoons chopped fresh parsley
100g white breadcrumbs
salt and freshly ground black pepper

Preheat the oven to 180°C/350°F/gas mark 4.

To make the stuffing, melt the butter and sauté the shallots without colouring. Add the chopped parsley, followed by the breadcrumbs and salt and pepper. Mix together well.

Stuff each quail, then close over the opening and secure with a small skewer. Place the quails on a baking tray, brush with a little olive oil and cook in the oven for 12–15 minutes, until they are golden brown.

Sweat the grapes in a pan with the knob of butter, while the quails are cooking.

Place a slice of foie gras on a slice of brioche, sit a quail on top and serve with hot grapes and their juice around the edge.

CANARD AU POIVRE VERT

The marriage of sweet succulent peas and peppercorns with their spicy bite works very well with rich duck. It's also great training for keeping peas and peppercorns on the right side of the fork! Have some baguette handy for when politeness gets too much for everyone and pushing and mopping take over.

For 2

2 duck legs
1 shallot, roughly chopped
1 garlic clove, peeled and crushed
olive oil
2 teaspoons marinated green peppercorns
300ml single cream
250g fresh green peas
salt and freshly ground black pepper

Preheat the oven to 190°C/375°F/gas mark 5.

In a roasting tin, set the duck legs on top of the shallot and garlic, pour over a little olive oil and cook for about 30 minutes.

Once the duck legs are done, remove from the tin and allow to rest while you make the sauce.

Skim off a little of the fat, then add the peppercorns and the cream directly to the tin, scraping the bottom to dislodge all the tasty sticky bits.

Put the tin on the hob and heat until the cream is bubbling and reduces. Add the peas and cook for a further 3 minutes, until they are tender.

Season and serve immediately.

VENISON WITH APPLE AND POTATO MASH & BLACKBERRY SAUCE

This is a wonderfully autumnal dish that mixes the best fruits of the season with tender, earthy venison – a great way of teaming three seasonal ingredients. It seems to be nature's trick to make things that are in season together, taste great together. It takes a bit of organisation to serve, because the sauce can only be made at the last minute, so I find it's best for just two as a treat.

For 2

2 venison steaks, 125g each
olive oil
300ml good beef stock
120g blackberry conserve
6–8 juniper berries
a sprig of fresh rosemary
20 blackberries

FOR THE APPLE AND POTATO MASH
4 eating apples, peeled, cored, cut into quarters and sliced
500g potatoes, peeled, boiled and crushed
salt and freshly ground black pepper

To make the mash, put the apples with 2 or 3 tablespoons of cold water into a saucepan with a tight-fitting lid. Cook until they are soft but still hold their shape.

Use a spoon to break up the apple slices, then stir them loosely through the mash. Season with salt and pepper.

Heat a heavy-bottomed frying pan. Rub the venison with a little oil and season. Fry the steaks for 2–3 minutes each side, then remove from the pan and allow them to rest.

Pour the stock into the pan, add the blackberry conserve, the juniper berries and rosemary and boil rapidly for up to 15 minutes, until it has reduced by two-thirds.

When the sauce has reduced, toss in the blackberries, allowing them to heat through and just soften in the sauce. Taste and adjust the seasoning if necessary.

Serve the venison on heated plates, drizzled with sauce and hot berries, accompanied by the apple and potato mash.

ROAST TURBOT WITH LINGUINE, COCKLES & MUSSELS

Often, on Sunday mornings when I'm expecting guests for lunch, I leave the house before anyone is up and drive to the magnificent market in the medieval town of Houdan, near Rouen. One of the fish stalls there is a makeshift huddle of trestle tables at the back of a refrigerated van that arrives direct from the harbour in Le Havre. The van is filled straight from the boats there, there has been no detour via the Parisian wholesale market of Rungis, so the fish is spanking fresh. Sunday lunches on those days are luxurious affairs, usually based around turbot or John Dory.

For 4

4 good fat slices of turbot, 150–200g each, on the bone, with its skin
3 tablespoons olive oil
80g butter
200g fresh linguine
2 shallots, finely chopped
400g cockles and mussels
zest and juice of 2 oranges
2–3 tablespoons double cream (optional)
fleur de sel and freshly ground black pepper

Heat the oven to 190°C/375°F/gas mark 5.

Place the fish in a baking tin with 2 tablespoons of the olive oil and half the butter. Cook for 15–20 minutes. To check that it's done, insert a knife at the backbone. If the flesh comes away easily and doesn't seem pink inside, it's ready.

While the fish is roasting, cook the pasta. Drain and keep warm. Toss with the remaining olive oil so the strands don't stick.

At the same time, sweat the shallots in the rest of the butter. Turn the heat up, throw in the cockles and mussels and give it all a good stir. Add the orange zest and juice and cover for a moment, then shake the pan and cook until the cockles and mussels open and release their juices.

Put the linguine into the pan with the cockles and mussels, stir in the cream and mix well, so the pasta is covered with the sauce. Season with salt and pepper, divide between individual plates and set the fish on top.

Serve immediately.

ROAST SALMON WITH MELTING CABBAGE, CHESTNUTS & BEURRE ROUGE

The French don't have such strict serving rules when it comes to red and white wine as we do in the UK. They don't think twice about serving red wine with fish, or indeed, white wine with meat. It really depends on how deeply flavoured the fish or meat is. For example, Condrieu is a white wine that goes very well with creamy chicken dishes. Salmon is a gutsy enough fish to happily team up with red wine, both in the glass and on the plate. Here it is served with a red wine *beurre blanc* – effectively a *beurre rouge*! Most of this dish can be prepared in advance and finished off just before serving. Using duck fat to cook the cabbage will give it a wonderfully musky, autumnal taste.

For 4–6

olive oil
1 shallot, finely chopped
1 litre stock
250ml good-quality red wine
50g duck fat
150g bacon chunks
1 smallish Savoy cabbage, chopped into 2cm chunks
20 cooked chestnuts, roughly chopped
1 whole salmon, approx. 1.5kg
salt and freshly ground black pepper
1 lemon, quartered
50–80g butter

Preheat the oven to 180°C/350°F/gas mark 4.

Heat a little oil in a saucepan, then add the shallot and sweat, without browning, for a few minutes until soft. Pour in the stock and the wine and simmer gently to reduce by two-thirds. Reserve until just before serving.

Melt the duck fat in a heavy-based frying pan. Add the bacon and the cabbage, stirring to make sure that the cabbage doesn't colour or burn. When the cabbage has wilted and cooked through until soft but still has a slight crunch, add the chestnuts and mix well. Reserve.

Place the salmon on foil on a baking tray. Brush with oil and sprinkle with a little sea salt.

Squeeze lemon juice into the cavity of the fish. Season with a little salt and pepper and pop the squeezed lemon in there too.

Put the fish in the oven and cook for about 20-30 minutes until cooked through. Lift the flesh at the spine with a sharp knife to check if it's cooked: when it comes away easily and there is no pinkish trace next to the bone, it's fine. Underdone is always slightly better than overdone with such a noble fish. (A fellow Irish cook, Agnes, gave me this tip, if you want to be more precise about your cooking times: allow 10 minutes per 2.5cm of thickness, measuring from the surface of the baking tray to the thickest part of the fish.)

While the fish is in the oven, reheat the cabbage and chestnuts and finish the sauce. Heat the wine and stock reduction, then whisk in the butter to make the sauce beautifully rich and give it a sheen.

Serve the fish whole at the table with the beurre rouge and cabbage on the side.

OYSTERS WITH FOIE GRAS & CHIVES

A true show-stopper of a recipe. Despite the luxurious-sounding ingredients, this is an easy and very convivial way to start a meal when teamed with a chilled glass of Champagne or Sancerre. The oysters are cooked fast on a bed of salt on a large tray and, really, that's all you need to do to serve them. Passed around or set within easy reach of all your guests, the hands-on element (not to mention the slurping) will help break the ice of even the most formal meal.

For 4–6

24 oysters
4 *biscottes*, or similar dried toast, finely crushed
salt
200g foie gras, raw or *mi-cuit* if you can find it
fresh chives, very finely chopped

Preheat the grill to its hottest setting. Shuck the oysters and reserve in a bowl, keeping the shells.

Cover a large baking tray with salt. The refined white variety will look better and cost less than the excellent *sel de Guérande*. It's simply for stabilising the oysters, so you'll be throwing it away afterwards.

Cut the foie gras into small cubes of about 1cm, then mix them with the crushed *biscottes* until they are coated on all sides. Drain the water from the oysters and place them back in their shells on the bed of salt.

Sprinkle the coated foie gras pieces evenly over the oysters and pop the tray under the grill for about 5 minutes or so, until you can see the oyster juices bubbling slightly.

Garnish with a few chopped chives and serve.

SEA BASS WITH GREENS

French people like the decorum of the formal dinner party, so for a typically French, posh evening that spoils your guests, go all out with a starter, a dessert and cheese course. To balance out the courses, go for a light main course such as this one. If you make sure that pudding and starter are firmly in the fridge, the main course is the only part of the meal you need to keep an eye on. With the greens and the fish coming fresh from the market, you can serve a light dish full of goodness and purity with the minimum of fuss.

For 4

4 nice sea bass fillets, 150–200g each, skins on
olive oil
fleur de sel and freshly ground black pepper
a knob of butter
1 shallot, very finely chopped
6–8 good handfuls of fresh greens, e.g. spinach or cabbage leaves, washed and drained
a handful of fresh chives, chopped
1 lemon, halved

Preheat the oven to 190°C/375°F/gas mark 5.

Set the fish on foil in a baking tin with a few drops of olive oil and a sprinkling of *fleur de sel*. Roast for about 7 minutes.

In a large shallow pan, heat some oil and butter. Gently sweat the shallot in the pan until soft and translucent. Throw the greens in, stir and cook until they are hot and wilted. Season to taste.

Serve immediately with the fish, the chopped chives, some more *fleur de sel* and a splash of lemon juice.

VERRINE OF SWEET POTATO & CRAB

Little layered dishes served in individual glasses or *verrines* have swept through France over the past couple of years. Following the trend for mini portions, which was itself started by the tapas craze, they are now on sale everywhere, from my *fromagerie* to my *pâtisserie*. And it's no wonder, as they are practical and pretty, and allow for all sorts of taste and texture combinations – hot or cold, cooked or raw, sweet or savoury. At home, they may take a little preparation and imagination but are so handy to serve. These ones, filled with a sweet potato purée and spicy crab, could be prepared completely and left to cool or served hot.

For 6

500g sweet potatoes, peeled, chopped and cooked
salt and freshly ground black pepper
1 avocado, peeled and diced
150g crab meat
zest and juice of 1 lime
1 level teaspoon cayenne pepper, *ras el-hanout* or other spice mix
olive oil

Pulse the sweet potato in a blender to make a smooth purée or simply mash with a fork. Season with salt and pepper.

Mix the avocado with the crab meat, lime juice and zest, spices and a little olive oil.

Fill the glasses two-thirds full with the sweet potato, then set some crab and avocado mixture on top.

LITTLE PARCELS OF BOUDIN BLANC WITH TRUFFLE OIL

Similar to Lancashire or Irish white pudding, *boudin blanc*, the bloodless, white version of *boudin noir*, is a sausage usually made with pork, pork fat or butter, and cream or milk, and is traditionally served around Christmas. It's thought to have originated from the boiled milk pudding eaten in the Middle Ages during *les fêtes*. Nowadays, much of the *boudin blanc* on offer has black truffle already speckled through it, but it will always benefit from a little drizzle of truffle oil to bump its flavour. If you can't find *boudin blanc*, use *boudin noir* or black pudding, frying or poaching some apples to add to the parcels before cooking.

For 6

250g *boudin blanc*
100g butter
5 sheets filo pastry
fresh chives, finely chopped
truffle oil

Preheat the oven to 190°C/375°F/gas mark 5.

Cut the *boudin* in half lengthways and then into chunks about 2cm long. Dry-fry them in a pan for about 5 minutes and reserve.

Melt the butter in the hot pan. Roll out the filo pastry and cut it into strips about 6cm wide. Brush each strip with melted butter, then place a piece of *boudin* and a sprinkling of chives at one end. Roll up the pastry with the *boudin* tightly held in the middle, pinching the edges. Put the parcels on a baking tray and cook for about 10 minutes, until they are golden.

Remove from the oven, drizzle with truffle oil and serve immediately.

CHAMPAGNE SUNDAES WITH MANDARIN ORANGES

A perfect little dessert to end rich dinners at Christmas time, this was created by fellow French food writer Keda Black, who is emblematic of the new, creative, adventurous French cook – her cookbooks with endless variations on French classics, like charlotte and pot au feu, have sold tens of thousands of copies. The bubbles from the Champagne and the freshness of the sorbet feel lovely on the palate. It makes a great alternative to the rich and buttery *bûche de Noël* that is traditionally served after turkey with chestnuts on Christmas Day. Don't worry about the rich and buttery amongst you, there a recipe for *bûche de Noël* on page 175.

For 6

1 orange
1 lemon
50g sugar
6 sheets gelatine
1 bottle Champagne
150ml whipping cream
6 mandarins
1 litre tub lemon or mandarin sorbet

Grate the zest from the orange and lemon and add to a saucepan with the sugar and 500ml of water. Set on a low heat and stir until the sugar has dissolved, making a light citrus syrup.

Soak the gelatine in cold water until it has softened, then squeeze out the excess water and dissolve in the warm syrup. Add 2 tablespoons of orange juice, stir and leave in the fridge for an hour or so, until it is just beginning to set.

Pour in 500ml of Champagne, stirring very lightly so it stays nice and fizzy. Put the jelly back in the fridge and leave until completely set.

Whip up the cream and chill.

Peel the mandarins and cut out their flesh with a sharp knife, moving the knife between the pithy separations of the segments.

Just before serving, make up individual sundae glasses. Start with a scoop of jelly, then some fruit, then the sorbet. Repeat the layers, topping the whole thing off with the whipped cream.

Serve right away, decorated with pieces of mandarin.

MILLEFEUILLE

Cancale is a town in Brittany that's known for many things: its oyster beds just off the main harbour, seafood, salty butter, and Breton biscuits. It seems like every other shop is a food shop, an *épicerie fine* selling Breton specialities. It's a beautiful place, with a lovely pier, a great market, and an oyster shack where you can sit eating your oysters, chucking your empty shells on to the beach like many people have done before you. The main reason I go there, however, is to visit the Grain de Vanille *pâtisserie*, owned by Olivier Roellinger, where one of the most famous *millefeuilles* in France is made.

The formula for this majestic *millefeuille* remains a very closely guarded secret. Olivier's masterpiece is made only twice a week, carefully timed for Sunday lunch and dinner as it stays flaky and light for only a few hours. The entire *pâtisserie* is geared to its assembly and distribution. Extra staff are taken on, room is made on the shelves. At precisely half past eleven, the morning version is lovingly assembled by the chef *pâtissier*. Two fat cushions of *crème pâtissière* speckled with Tahitian vanilla seeds (two pods per litre of milk, an expensive exercise!) and 'lightened' with whipped Normandy cream are piped between three dark toffee-coloured puff pastry oblongs, baked the day before. Icing sugar is sprinkled on top then melted golden with a blow torch – a far cry from the usual caramel layer that other chefs let cook directly onto the pastry, hardening it. The final touch is a swirl of dried vanilla pod, then the cake is carefully placed in its box. Outside, the queue of those who have placed their orders (and there are never any leftovers for last-minute decisions) winds expectantly around the corner of the building as the church bells call them to come to confess their gluttony.

The cake is definitely too labour-intensive to try at home. I prefer to undo the elements for my guests and serve them separately – a deconstructed version that you'll find on page 178. But if you're ever in the area for a few days, placing your order and queuing around the block is the only thing to do...

CAFÉ GOURMAND

This is the dessert I often serve when my French girlfriends come round for lunch. Their palates might be crying out for something sweet but their consciences will only allow them a tiny bite. I make life exceptionally easy for myself by making the mousse and buying the chocolate morsels, which can be mini chocolate cakes or dark chocolate macaroons. This way my girlfriends love me for catering to their waistlines rather than their appetites!

For 4

80g good-quality dark chocolate
3 medium eggs, separated
4 mini chocolate cakes (e.g. brownies) or dark chocolate macaroons
4 very good cups of espresso

Break the chocolate into pieces and melt it in a heatproof bowl over a pan of simmering water or in the microwave. Remove from the heat.

Add the egg yolks one by one, beating as you go.

Whisk the egg whites in a clean bowl until they are firm and fold them gently into the chocolate mixture with a metal spoon.

Pour the mousse into individual glasses or cups and leave to set in the fridge for 2–3 hours. Make up a mini plate for each guest, with a mini mousse and a macaroon, and serve with an espresso.

TOTALLY CHOCOLATE TARTE

Even after a long, drawn-out aperitif, even after a substantial dinner, even after a satisfying tour de France cheese course, most people still crave something sweet. And sometimes only chocolate will do, which is why it's vital to have a few of the richest chocolate recipes up your sleeve. Portions can be small, but must be packed with intense flavour. This *tarte* fits the bill perfectly – it's chocolate from the first crumb to the last!

For 6–8

FOR THE CHOCOLATE PASTRY
250g plain flour
100g icing sugar
1 tablespoon cocoa powder
200g butter, very cold, cut into pieces
2 egg yolks, lightly beaten with 1 tablespoon water

FOR THE CHOCOLATE CREAM FILLING
200ml double cream
300g best-quality dark chocolate
3 egg yolks
40g unsalted butter

Preheat the oven to 190°C/375°F/gas mark 5.

To make the pastry, put all the dry ingredients in a food processor with the butter. Whizz for a minute or so until the mixture resembles fine breadcrumbs, then make a well in the centre and pour in the egg yolks. Bring together with a wooden spoon and press with your hands to form a ball. Cover in cling film and chill in the fridge for at least 2 hours before using.

Roll the pastry out on a cool surface and use it to line either a circular tin 28cm in diameter or a similar sized rectangular tin. Prick the pastry base with a fork.

Cook in the oven for 15–20 minutes, until it is crispy around the edges. Remove and cool completely before filling.

To make the filling, heat the cream until it's almost (but not quite) boiling. Break the chocolate into pieces in a heatproof bowl, then pour over the cream and stir well. Add the egg yolks and butter and stir again.

Pour the mixture into the pastry case and chill for 3–4 hours until it is set.

Home baking is less of a national hobby in France than it is in Ireland. A French cook wouldn't spend entire afternoons producing traybakes, scones and sponge cakes to stock up for coffee mornings and afternoon teas. This, of course, is because entertaining happens mostly around 'real' meals – lunch or dinner – rather than quick cups of tea or coffee snatched from the day. And with a *boulangerie-pâtisserie* seemingly at every corner of even the tiniest French village, the French home cook rarely sees the point of trying to replicate the skills of a pastry chef. There is no shame attached to producing shop-bought cakes for pudding at home. Choosing wisely, making the effort to travel to a good *pâtissier* and perhaps even ordering his speciality are considered just as skilful and caring towards guests as spending hours making them an elaborate cake.

For the professionals, pastry making is considered a very separate discipline. Many chefs see desserts as a bit of an afterthought, an optional extra, not the creative hub of a restaurant meal. Conversely, in the more expensive places, there will be dedicated pastry chef. Here, desserts are treated with the respect I think they deserve and a procession of pre-desserts, a couple of substantial ones and then perhaps also some *petits fours* can quickly cover your table!

If, like me, you always look at the list of desserts on a menu before anything else, planning your meal backwards to make sure you will have enough room at the end, this chapter is key. I have included the great feast cakes, such as *bûche de Noël* and *galette des rois*, for when you are feeling ambitious. There is a recipe for the substantial *far Breton*, which will keep for days and loves being taken on picnics. *Tartes* figure prominently, of course, alongside many other fruit-based puddings, allowing you to follow the seasons. Lastly, there are a few ideas that could easily have been housed in the POSH chapter and, I hope, might awaken the dormant pastry chef in anyone with a seriously sweet tooth.

SWEET

TARTE AUX FRAMBOISES

A little effort is required here to achieve *pâtisserie*-level presentation. It's amazing what some clever placing of raspberries and a light dusting of icing sugar will do, though, if your pastry base is less than neat. Taste-wise, there can be no short cuts with the shortcrust, I'm afraid. It's homemade or not at all! In fact, along with the flavour of fresh raspberries, it's really what this dessert is all about, the crumbling, buttery, sweet shortcrust acting as a canvas for tart fruit smoothed through the palate by rich vanilla *crème pâtissière*. It can all be prepared well beforehand and assembled just before your guests arrive. Don't leave it any more than a couple of hours before serving, or the pastry will go soggy under the cream.

For 6–8

500g fresh raspberries
icing sugar (optional), for serving

FOR THE SWEET SHORTCRUST PASTRY
250g plain flour
2 teaspoons sugar or, much better, vanilla sugar
a pinch of *fleur de sel*
125g very cold unsalted butter, cut into small cubes

FOR THE CRÈME PÂTISSIÈRE
400ml whole milk
1 vanilla pod, split in half
5 large egg yolks
100g sugar
50g plain flour, sifted

To make the sweet shortcrust pasty, sift the flour into a bowl, add the sugar and salt and mix. Drop in the butter and work it into the flour with the tips of your fingers. Lift up the mixture as much as possible, so that air gets in, to make the pastry crumbly and light.

When the mixture resembles fine breadcrumbs, make a well in the centre and pour in a couple of tablespoonfuls of very cold water. Mix it in quickly, kneading with your fingers and then your hands to make a ball of pastry. Cover the ball with cling film and chill in the freezer for 30 minutes or in the fridge for an hour or so.

Remove the pastry and roll it out into a circle large enough to line a 20 or 22cm non-stick tart base (there will be a little left over). Put the base in the fridge for 30 minutes or in the freezer for 15 minutes.

Heat the oven to 200°C/400°F/gas mark 6. Prick the base of the tart with a fork to stop it puffing up, then line with baking parchment. Fill it with baking beans and cook for 15 minutes or so, until the edges of the pastry are golden. Remove the baking beans. At this stage you could put it back in the oven for 5 minutes or so if you feel the middle has not cooked sufficiently, but it's usually fine. Let the base cool right down.

Meanwhile, make the *crème pâtissière* by heating the milk in a saucepan with the halved vanilla pod. Bring to the boil but don't let it boil over. As the milk is heating, whisk the egg yolks with the sugar until they are pale and creamy and have doubled in volume. Add the flour and mix well.

Pour the hot milk on to the egg yolks, whisking well. Pour the custard back into the saucepan and slowly heat it again, whisking all the time to get rid of any little lumps of flour, until it thickens. Keep whisking for about 2 minutes – it will be cooked when it turns slightly liquid again (if it isn't cooked, you will taste the flour rather than the eggs and vanilla). Take it off the heat, pour into a bowl and let it cool completely.

Spoon the cooled *crème pâtissière* into the tart base and smooth it out evenly. Set the raspberries neatly and tightly packed on to it, discarding any whose juice leaks out. Dredge with icing sugar just before serving, if you like.

STRAWBERRY PEACH SUNDAES

This dish is a take on the ever popular trifle. It's the perfect candidate for serving in little *verrines* or pretty glasses. It's fresh, sweet and cool. If your meal goes on a bit and these sundaes are waiting for you in the fridge, the biscuits get a little soaking and the layers merge into each other, making it even more delicious.

For 4

16 Amaretti biscuits
Amaretto or crème de pêche liqueur
600ml double cream, whipped
4 peaches, skin removed and sliced
300g strawberries, washed and hulled

Crush the biscuits and sprinkle them into the bottom of each glass. They should come about a third of the way up.

Pour over the liqueur, then add a spoonful of whipped cream. Next come the peach slices, followed by another dollop of cream.

Whizz the strawberries in a blender until they are smooth and finish by pouring them over the cream.

ÎLES FLOTTANTES AUX PRALINES ROSES

A praline is a sugar-coated almond which can be coloured and flavoured. When it is crushed into a powder, it becomes the *pralin* used in cakes and desserts. Mixed with chocolate, its name changes again, to *praliné*. Pink *pralines roses* are most famously used in *tarte aux pralines*, a dessert from Lyon, and *brioche aux pralines*. The pink colouring prettily seeps into the fluffy brioche and the almonds give a satisfying crunch. Much the same thing happens in this recipe, where you can make the most of the pink sweets by crumbling them into the meringue as you cook it, adding them to the *crème anglaise* or simply sprinkling them over the dish before serving.

For 4

125g sugar, plus two tablespoons
5 eggs, separated
500ml whole milk
4 tablespoons *pralines roses*

Beat the 125g of sugar with the egg yolks in a bowl until they're pale and white, and doubled in size.

Bring the milk to the boil in a saucepan, then pour on to the yolks, stirring well. Put the custard back into the saucepan and heat, stirring continuously with a wooden spoon. When it thickens, take it off the heat and let it cool right down.

Beat the egg whites with the remaining sugar until they are as stiff as meringues. With a metal spoon, make little mounds about 5cm across. These can now be poached in barely simmering milk or simply cooked in the microwave, on a glass plate, on high for about 30 seconds. As soon as the meringue starts to swell, stop cooking. Let them cool.

To serve, float the islands in a sea of custard, either in individual bowls or a large one, and crumble the pralines over the dishes.

TARTE FINE AUX POMMES

In traditional *pâtisseries*, it is the *tarte fine aux pommes* that separates the boys from the men. *Pâtissiers* pride themselves on their *tarte* being the finest it can be. Worlds away from a rustic, richly filled, pastry-covered *tourte*, *'la fine'* must be thin, while the layers remain distinct. First your teeth bite through melting slivers of roasted apples, which are set into a soft spread of apple purée. Then they hit the crunch of puff pastry, often slightly caramelised around the edge by the sweet juice of the apples. Everything must look neat and tidy, of course, so a little construction effort is required. I'm not suggesting that you make your own puff pastry, but if you are using ready-rolled do get your rolling pin out and make the *tarte* base as thin as possible.

For 4

4 Granny Smith apples
1 packet good ready-rolled puff pastry
1 egg yolk, beaten, or a little milk
50g butter (I like to use salted butter here), melted, plus extra for greasing
4 tablespoons sugar

Peel, core and slice two of the apples. Put them in a saucepan with a tablespoon of cold water and cover with a tight-fitting lid. Place on a gentle heat and stew until the apples have disintegrated, then leave to cool completely.

Preheat the oven to 160°C/325°F/gas mark 3.

Roll out the pastry thinly and cut into two rectangles. Place on a buttered baking sheet, then run a knife around the edges about 1cm in to make a border, but don't cut through the pastry completely.

Divide the apple purée over the two rectangles and spread smoothly from the centre of the pastry out to the border.

Peel, quarter and core the remaining apples, then slice them very finely in regular half-moon shapes. Arrange the slices over the purée as evenly as possible, overlapping them and lining them up with the border on the pastry.

Brush the exposed pastry with some beaten egg yolk or a little milk.

Brush the melted butter over the apples, sprinkle over the sugar and cook in the oven for about 15 minutes, until the pastry is risen and golden and the apples are slightly caramelised.

Serve warm with crème fraîche or good vanilla ice cream.

GALETTES DES ROIS

Every year, just as everyone is getting over the excesses of Christmas and New Year, the bakers and *pâtissiers* of France assail the population with flat, shiny *galettes des rois*. Filled with frangipane, encased in rich puff pastry, it seems impossible anyone would want to tuck into them so soon after *bûche de Noël* and turkey with chestnuts. It is perhaps the ritual more than the cake that has people hooked, for the cutting and serving of the *galette* is turned into an elaborate scenario.

The first time I encountered it, I truly believed that it was a joke at my expense, unsuspecting foreigner that I was. The *galette* was cut into eleven pieces (one more than the number of guests) then I was sent under the table to call out everyone's name and thus impartially decide the order in which everyone got their slice. The secrecy is necessary for the stakes are high. Inside each *galette* is a *fève*, a little charm. First served in Roman times, whoever came across it in his piece of cake was crowned king of the party. The tradition is still going strong, although *galettes* are now served at Epiphany and the *fèves* have become little porcelain figurines, passionately collected by *fabophiles*.

It has become the customary way for families, companies, town halls and schools to gather and celebrate the new year all through the month of January. Bakers and *pâtissiers* always include cardboard crowns with the cake, some of which are objects of great beauty and, just as with the *bûche de Noël*, can be designed by artists or fashion designers for the more famous shops. Nowadays the king or queen gets to choose his or her corresponding co-monarch from around the table and wins the honour of inviting everyone for the next *galette*. The extra slice is '*la part du pauvre*' or the poor man's share, given in the past to those who would beg for food. Nowadays it is given to the greediest guest who wants second helpings. This is rarely the case in my house, for amongst my rather competitive children, it seems the lure of the prize and ensuing coronation is more attractive than the cake itself. All eyes are rooted on my knife as I cut up the *galette*, checking to see if it should go 'clink' as it cuts into something hard and give away the mystery.

GALETTE DES ROIS

This cake is served at Epiphany, the 'Kings' in its name referring to the Three Kings who followed the star to Bethlehem. For the *fève* to determine who becomes king or queen of your table (see previous page) you could use a small dried bean, as the Romans did (the name has come down from the Latin for 'bean'), or the now traditional tiny china figure, or you could just as easily use a coin.

For 6

50g butter, softened
2 eggs
50g caster sugar
1 tablespoon plain flour
50g ground almonds
a few drops of good-quality bitter almond extract
a pinch of salt
1 tablespoon rum (optional)
1 packet good puff pastry
1 *fève*
1 egg, lightly beaten

Preheat the oven to 180°C/350°F/gas mark 4.

Line a large baking sheet with baking parchment and set it aside.

The puff pastry should be defrosted but kept in the fridge until the last minute to ensure that it rises properly.

In a bowl mix the butter, 2 eggs, sugar and flour until well combined. Add the ground almonds, mix well, then add the bitter almond extract, the salt and the rum, if using.

Roll out the puff pastry and cut two 22cm rounds. Place one on the baking sheet (leave the other in the fridge for now). Scoop the almond cream into the centre of the pastry and gently distribute it evenly across, leaving a 2cm rim uncovered.

Place the *fève* anywhere you like on the almond cream, then brush the uncovered rim with beaten egg.

Remove the second puff pastry round from the fridge and gently place it on top of the almond cream, aligning the edges so that they sit directly over those of the lower round. Without pushing the almond cream out, gently bring the edges down to just touch the lower ones, pinching the edges together gently to make them stick together.

Brush the remaining beaten egg over the top of the puff pastry to glaze it, then make a small hole in the centre with knife. Gently score the pastry to make a criss-cross pattern, being careful not to cut all the way through.

Bake for 10 minutes, then reduce the oven temperature to 160°C/325°F/gas mark 3, and bake for another 20 minutes, or until lightly golden and the pastry has puffed up.

Let it cool completely before cutting.

FAR BRETON AUX PRUNEAUX

Along with *kouig amam,* this is Brittany's most emblematic cake. A robust confection of sweet crêpe batter studded with juicy prunes and flavoured with rum, it matches the equally robust Breton climate and is great to take on windy picnics. It is, of course, just as good served at the end of a meal or in slices with a cup of tea or coffee.

For 4–6

150g plain flour
125g sugar
4 eggs, beaten
500ml whole milk
a dash of rum
200g pitted prunes
1 egg yolk, beaten

Preheat the oven to 180°C/350°F/gas mark 4.

Sift the flour into a bowl, add the sugar and mix. Make a well in the centre, add the 4 eggs and whisk vigorously until the batter is smooth.

Pour the milk in little by little, whisking all the time. Add the rum.

Butter the inside of a 20 x 22 or 24cm gratin dish. Pour the batter in and scatter the prunes though it, pushing them under the surface slightly. Cook for 30 minutes in the oven.

Remove from the oven, brush the top of the *far* with the beaten egg yolk and cook for another 25–30 minutes, until the top is nice and golden.

Serve warm with crème fraîche.

PLUM & CHERRY VANILLA COMPOTE

Surely the purest and simplest way of making pudding out of seasonal fruit. The mix of these two works beautifully, with the softness of the vanilla setting their taste off to perfection. In my country kitchen, I always dreamt of stocking up fruit preserves and compotes in those wonderful Le Parfait jars, but somehow the fruit always got eaten too fast!

For 4

12 red plums
200g plump ripe cherries
sugar to taste
1 vanilla pod, split

Wash the fruit, remove the stalks and place in a saucepan with a splash of water, the split vanilla pod and some sugar. Heat very gently and simmer until the fruit releases its juice and softens. Remove from the heat and let the vanilla infuse.

Serve hot, warm or cold with custard, fresh cream or clotted cream and shortbread or almond biscuits.

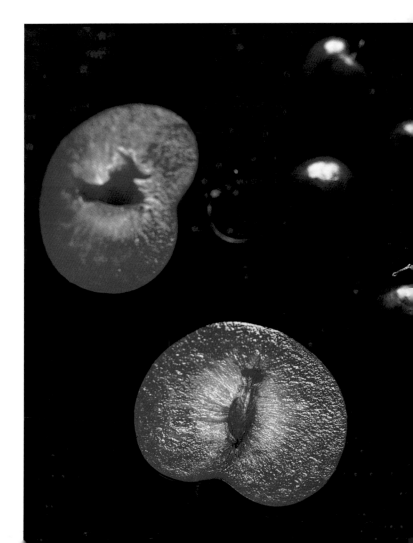

MILK CREAMS WITH ROSE & CARDAMOM

Rose and cardamom are two fragrances that stem from Tunisian and Moroccan cuisine. Pierre Hermé, the famous *pâtissier* who has had such an influence on French desserts and sweets over the last few years, uses rose in one of his most famous cakes, making rose-flavoured desserts very popular. Here is one of my own – delicate and simple to make, these creams are pretty summer desserts.

For 6

1 litre whole milk
2 tablespoons sugar
½ teaspoon ground cardamom
a few drops of rosewater
rose petals (or almonds or pistachios), to decorate

Bring the milk to the boil in a saucepan and simmer for about 10 minutes, or until the volume has reduced by about a third.

Add the sugar and simmer for a further 10 minutes.

Leave to cool before adding the cardamom and the rosewater. Pour into glasses and leave to chill completely (2–3 hours) before serving.

BRIOCHE PERDUE WITH BLACKBERRY SAUCE

This is a richer, fluffier version of French toast. My convalescence dish as a child, it was simultaneously welcomed and dreaded, because it signalled that my appetite had returned but also that I would soon be back at school.

Just like bread and butter pudding, it has enjoyed a revival in France over the past few years as all types of comfort food find their way on to even the most chic of restaurant menus. And yes, it is best to forget the humble using-up-stale-bread origin of this dessert and buy the freshest brioche you can find.

For 4

200g fresh or frozen blackberries
2–3 tablespoons icing sugar
2 eggs
50ml whole milk
4 thick slices fresh brioche
75g butter
icing sugar or granulated sugar, for serving

In a saucepan, poach the blackberries in just a little water. Add icing sugar to taste. Reserve.

Beat the eggs into the milk, then pour into a wide bowl. Dip the slices of brioche in the eggy milk for a minute or so. You want them to soak up the liquid but not fall apart.

Heat the butter in a frying pan and fry the brioche until crispy and golden on both sides.

Dredge with icing sugar, or sprinkle with granulated sugar if you prefer the crunch, and serve immediately with the warm poached blackberries.

BÛCHE DE NOËL

Just like Christmas pudding, Christmas log is one you should try at home at least once. It's a great recipe to do with kids and this dinky version should appeal to them even more. Quantities are generous in case of any slip ups, and the butter icing hides a million sins.

There are lots of versions these days, from iced logs to meringues. Every Christmas, the famous *pâtissiers* of Paris rival each other with special, limited edition *bûches de Noël*. In the past, Karl Lagerfeld has designed one with candied fruit and encrusted jewels, and Philippe Stark developed a wood-flavoured one. The more traditional version below, with sponge and buttercream, is easiest to make at home.

For 6

3 eggs
75g caster sugar
50g plain flour, sifted
25g cocoa powder, sifted
100g dark chocolate, melted, to decorate

FOR THE ICING
100g unsalted butter, softened
100g icing sugar, sifted
1 dessertspoon Grand Marnier
50g cocoa powder
3–4 tablespoons chestnut purée

Preheat the oven to 190°C/375°F/gas mark 5. Whisk the eggs and sugar together until they are thick and creamy, then fold the flour and cocoa powder into the mixture using a metal spoon.

Line a Swiss roll tin with greaseproof paper. Pour the mixture into the tin and smooth over with a spatula. Bake for 10–12 minutes until firm to the touch. Turn out the sponge, leaving the greaseproof paper in place, and cool on a wire tray. Once cooled and still on the greaseproof paper, working from the very edges of the sponge, cut out as many circles as possible with a scone or cookie cutter.

For the icing, cream together the butter and icing sugar with an electric whisk. Add the Grand Marnier, then the cocoa powder, beating as you go. Finally add the chestnut purée and mix thoroughly.

CONSTRUCTION
Cut out a piece of cardboard the same width as the sponge circles and about one and a half times their length when they are stacked together. Cover it with silver or gold foil. With a butter knife, spread icing on one side of the first disc of sponge. Set it on the work surface, icing side up. Place the next piece on top and continue to build a pillar of sandwiched cake discs.

Turn the pillar on its side. Put a little icing on the board and use it to anchor the cake. Spread the remainder of the icing all over and smooth it down with a flat knife (have some hot water and kitchen paper next to you to clean and dry the knife as you go). Run a fork all over the cake to give the effect of a log.

DECORATION
With a dessertspoon, drip the chocolate on to greaseproof paper in the shape of a Christmas tree and leave it in a cool place (not the fridge). Once hardened, remove the greaseproof paper and stick the tree on to the top of the log.

Before serving, leave in a cool place, in a closed cake tin if possible, but again not the fridge, as the condensation will spoil the icing.

STRAWBERRY MILLEFEUILLE GONE TO PIECES

I could be slightly pompous and call this deconstructed, but really it's pudding made easier, not intellectual. There are many French classic cakes which, to my mind, belong solely in the hands of a pastry chef and should not be attempted at home. When you have experienced *millefeuille* perfection à la Olivier Roellinger in Cancale (see page 153), you'll see what I mean about this particular sweet masterpiece. Breaking up the elements gives you more freedom to play with the proportions in each mouthful, keeping the individual tastes defined.

For 4

1 packet good ready-rolled puff pastry
50g butter, melted
250g strawberries, washed and hulled
icing sugar, to serve

FOR THE CRÈME PÂTISSIÈRE
5 egg yolks
100g sugar
1 tablespoon plain flour
1 vanilla pod, split in half
300ml whole milk

Preheat the oven to 180°C/350°F/gas mark 4.

First make the *crème pâtissière* by whisking the egg yolks with the sugar and flour in a bowl until the mixture is pale and fluffy and has doubled in volume.

Pour the milk into a saucepan and bring to the boil with the vanilla pod. Pour on to the egg yolks, stirring well. Then put the whole lot back into the saucepan and heat again, stirring continuously.

When the cream thickens, let it cook very gently for a minute or two, then remove from the heat and let it cool completely. Leave the vanilla pod in for extra flavour.

Roll out the puff pastry and brush with melted butter. Cut into long strips and twist them, then put them on a baking sheet and cook until golden brown. Remove from the oven and leave to cool.

Make up little glasses of strawberries with some *crème pâtissière* on top and serve the pastry twists next to them, dredged in icing sugar.

MEERT WAFFLES

The French word *gaufre* translates as waffle, a rather clumsy name for the delicate little wafers that are made in the Meert *pâtisserie*. These waffles take the meaning of *gaufre* to another realm; they seem to have distilled all the sweetness and thickness of a normal sized waffle into a mini version, wrapped in monogrammed golden paper and set snugly in exquisite pink-lined boxes. They are a far cry from the thick fluffy lattices, smothered in whipped cream and chocolate sauce, served in many French tea salons.

The beautiful Meert *pâtisserie* and *salon de thé* is the pride of Lille in the north of France. It's the oldest *confiserie* in town, a sweet shop decorated with ancient plaster-work, old labels, drawings and antique cake boxes. Established in 1761 as a sweet shop, it was the *chocolatier* Rollez who gave the original shop its flamboyant look in 1839 and created the first of the famous thin waffles, filled with vanilla flavoured buttercream, which were to become the favourite sweet treat of General de Gaulle.

And they *are* impossibly sweet. The soft, toasted biscuit holding in the buttercream does little to counteract the sugary, buttery layer that squeezes out when you bite into the waffle. Somehow, the flavour isn't overwhelmed by the sugar, however, and the intense vanilla taste wins through. Perhaps it has something to do with the fineness of the icing sugar, ground from granulated sugar on the premises by the *pâtissiers* of today according to the original recipe. Meert have not extended their production, and the *gaufres* are hard to come by. In Paris, they are sold at the Grande Epicerie du Bon Marché, Paris's most prestigious food hall. But not every day, as stocks soon run out. As with many of France's regional delicacies, you must make the journey to them instead of hoping they can come to you. No matter how much in demand they may be, respecting quality and tradition is everything. I have given up buying them, as I cannot just eat the one. If you have a seriously sweet tooth, you're hooked forever.

ALMOND ICE CREAM WITH ORANGE SOUP

A refreshing dessert with Spanish influences, it takes a little meticulous preparation but then will behave itself in the fridge until you need it. If you can't find almond ice cream, use hazelnut or vanilla.

For 4

10–12 juicy oranges
150ml white wine
75g sugar
2 teaspoons cornflour
juice of 1 lemon
almond ice cream
Grand Marnier (optional)
toasted almond flakes or almond biscuits

Peel the oranges and remove their flesh with a sharp knife, slipping in and out of the segments. Do this over a large bowl to collect all the juice.

Heat the wine, dissolve the sugar in it and simmer for about 15 minutes.

Mix the cornflour with a little water and pour into the wine syrup. Add the orange segments and orange and lemon juice. Heat gently for 2–3 minutes, so the orange segments disintegrate slightly.

Leave to cool, then chill. Add a splash of Grand Marnier if you like.

Serve in pretty glasses with scoops of ice cream and some toasted almond flakes or almond biscuits.

TOMATO TATIN

There are so many versions of the *tarte Tatin*, and with this one I am challenging you to see tomatoes not as a vegetable, but as a fruit. Ever since master *pâtissier* Pierre Hermé introduced his celebrated tomato and strawberry salad, the French have taken to doing just that.

For 6

80g caster sugar
50g butter
a pinch of salt
1 tablespoon olive oil
8 nice medium tomatoes, halved and seeds removed
25g semolina flour
1 packet good ready-rolled puff pastry

Preheat the oven to 200°C/400°F/gas mark 6. Place the sugar in a baking dish or a heavy-based ovenproof pan with 2 tablespoons of water and heat slowly. Once the sugar has dissolved, bring it to a lively bubble and leave it for about 5 minutes, without stirring, until it caramelises. It will start around the edges of the pan – as soon as you see this, lift the pan and swirl the syrup around to help it caramelise evenly, before placing it back on the heat again. When it's a uniform, light brown colour, add the butter and salt and stir gently as it melts. Remove the caramel from the heat.

Heat the olive oil in a sauté pan, then add the tomatoes, flesh side down, and cook for about 5 minutes. Evenly distribute the tomatoes, flesh side down, in the baking dish with the caramel and sprinkle with the semolina flour, then place the rolled out pastry dough on top, tucking the edges in. Cook in the centre of the oven for about 25 minutes, until golden brown.

Remove from the oven and let it stand for 5 minutes, then turn it upside down on to a serving plate, scraping out the caramel and juices from the bottom of the dish. Serve with crème fraîche.

BANANA MANGO TATIN

The *tarte Tatin* or upside-down tart has seen a real resurgence in France over the past few years. The wonderful thing about it is that you can make it with lots of different fruits. Dried mango goes really well with bananas, creating an interesting texture, as long as you use the plump sliced dried mango (no leathery slices please). Of course, if you can find a delicious ripe mango, one that's not too juicy, that would do just fine as well.

For 6–8

150g caster sugar
50g salted butter
3–4 bananas
6–8 slices soft dried mango
1 packet good ready-rolled puff pastry

Preheat the oven to 180°C/350°F/gas mark 4.

Place the sugar in a baking dish or a heavy-based ovenproof pan with 2 tablespoons of water and heat slowly. Once the sugar has dissolved, bring it to a lively bubble and leave it for about 5 minutes, without stirring, until it caramelises. It will start around the edges of the pan – as soon as you see this, lift the pan and swirl the syrup around to help it caramelise evenly, before placing it back on the heat again. When it's a uniform, light brown colour, add the butter and stir gently as it melts. Remove the caramel from the heat.

Cut the bananas in 3cm rounds and place in the caramel, followed by the mango slices. Place the puff pastry over the caramel and tuck the edges in, as if you were making a bed. Put in the oven for 25–30 minutes, just until the pastry is evenly golden.

Remove from the oven and let it stand for 5 minutes before turning it upside down on to a serving dish. Serve with crème fraîche.

CONVERSION CHARTS

Weight (solids)

7g	¼oz
10g	½oz
20g	¾oz
25g	1oz
40g	1½oz
50g	2oz
60g	2½oz
75g	3oz
100g	3½oz
110g	4oz (¼lb)
125g	4½oz
150g	5½oz
175g	6oz
200g	7oz
225g	8oz (½lb)
250g	9oz
275g	10oz
300g	10½oz
310g	11oz
325g	11½oz
350g	12oz (¾lb)
375g	13oz
400g	14oz
425g	15oz
450g	1lb
500g (0.5kg)	1lb 2oz
600g	1¼lb
700g	1½lb
750g	1lb 10oz
900g	2lb
1kg	2¼lb
1.1kg	2½lb
1.2kg	2lb 12oz
1.3kg	3lb
1.5kg	3lb 5oz
1.6kg	3½lb
1.8kg	4lb
2kg	4lb 8oz
2.25kg	5lb
2.5kg	5lb 8oz
3kg	6lb 8oz

Volume (liquids)

5ml	1 teaspoon
10ml	1 dessertspoon
15ml	1 tablespoon or ½fl oz
30ml	1fl oz
40ml	1½fl oz
50ml	2fl oz
60ml	2½fl oz
75ml	3fl oz
100ml	3½fl oz
125ml	4fl oz
150ml	5fl oz (¼ pint)
160ml	5½fl oz
175ml	6fl oz
200ml	7fl oz
225ml	8fl oz
250ml (0.25 litre)	9fl oz
300ml	10fl oz (½ pint)
325ml	11fl oz
350ml	12fl oz
370ml	13fl oz
400ml	14fl oz
425ml	15fl oz (¾ pint)
450ml	16fl oz
500ml (0.5 litre)	18fl oz
550ml	19fl oz
600ml	20fl oz (1 pint)
700ml	1¼ pints
850ml	1½ pints
1 litre	1¾ pints
1.2 litres	2 pints
1.5 litres	2½ pints
1.8 litres	3 pints
2 litres	3½ pints

Length

5mm	¼ inch
1cm	½ inch
2cm	¾ inch
2.5cm	1 inch
3cm	1¼ inch
4cm	1½ inch
5cm	2 inches
7.5 cm	3 inches
10cm	4 inches
15cm	6 inches
18cm	7 inches
20cm	8 inches
25cm	10 inches
28cm	11 inches
30 cm	12 inches

Oven temperatures

110°C	225°F	gas mark ¼	cool
120°C	250°F	gas mark ½	cool
130°C	275°F	gas mark 1	very low
150°C	300°F	gas mark 2	very low
160°C	325°F	gas mark 3	low
180°C	350°F	gas mark 4	moderate
190°C	375°F	gas mark 5	mod. hot
200°C	400°F	gas mark 6	hot
220°C	425°F	gas mark 7	hot
230°C	450°F	gas mark 8	very hot
240°C	475°F	gas mark 9	very hot

* For fan-assisted ovens, reduce temperatures by 10°C/50°F

Temperature conversion
$C = 5/9 (F-32)$
$F = 9/5C + 32$

INDEX